The Kid's Guide to Collecting

Statehood Quarters

and Other Cool Coins!

Kevin Flynn, Ron Volpe, and Kelsey Flynn

Whitman Coin Books

St. Martin's Griffin ☙ New York

Photos used by permission of Kevin Flynn and Whitman Coin Books

www.stmartins.com

ISBN 1-58238-099-6

First published in the United States under the title of *Those Amazing Coins* by Kevin Flynn and Ron Volpe

First St. Martin's Griffin Edition: November 2000

10   9   8   7   6   5   4   3   2   1

Also by Kevin Flynn

The Kid's Statehood Quarters Collector's Folder

Contents

Acknowledgments

Thanks to Kenneth Bressett for writing the foreword for this book. Ken has been helping the hobby for years by sharing information and teaching others. He leads with his actions so that others will follow and learn.

Thank you also to Tony Boccuti, Melissa Boccuti, Matthew Flynn, and Kelsey Flynn for helping with the front cover and to Melissa Bocciti for writing a section.

To J. T. Stanton, Bill Fivaz, Sam Lukes, John Wexler, Alan Meghrig, Bill Van Note, William Afanato, Jim Lafferty, Craig Sholley, Tony Boccuti, John Bordner, William Murray Jr., Bruce Hickmott, and Brian Raines go thanks for supplying some of the coins and/or information for this book. These individuals are always willing to lend a hand when needed and do so for the benefit of the hobby.

We would like to thank Beth Deisher of *Coin World;* Dave Harper of *Numismatic News;* Mike Gumpel, Rudy Bahr, Gail Baker, Kelly Swett, Robert Hoge, and Stephen Bobbitt of the American Numismatic Association; and the United States Mint for its help with the Washington State Quarters and other information.

Finally, we would like to thank Mrs. Croker and her fourth-grade class for reviewing this book and offering their comments. We would especially like to thank Veran Drenik for the artwork and editing she provided. We would like to thank Donna Brophy for editing.

Foreword by
Kenneth Bressett,
Past President American
Numismatic Association

I have had an interest in collecting coins for more than sixty years. When I started looking for coins in my change, it was easy to find just about every date and mintmark for everything as far back as 1892. It was exciting to find any coin worth more than face value, but the real thrill was to complete each set or trade with others for missing pieces.

This book has been written for a beginning collector. It has in it everything needed for a child to get started and to continue on for years of enjoyment. It is exactly the kind of book I wanted when I started collecting; unfortunately, there were no such books back then.

In this book, you will get clear answers to all of the questions that any beginner needs to know. Written in a style that is easy to understand, it emphasizes the enjoyment and fun of coin collecting. Best of all, it has been written by both an expert on the subject and his young daughter, who is equally enthusiastic about the hobby.

You will learn a lot about coins in this book. You will also learn about the history of this great country, the artistry of designs used on American money, the different kinds of metals used in these coins, and how to appreciate the value of these rare and unusual treasures that so often pass unnoticed through the hands of the general public. It may well be the beginning of an adventure that will last for the rest of your life. I hope that it is and that you enjoy your excursion into coin collecting as much as I have.

From a Kid's View
by Kelsey Flynn

Coins are very interesting and one of my favorite hobbies, although soccer is my *favorite activity*. I have two coin books, and I enjoy looking at them and showing them to my friends at school and at the pool in the summer. (But I have to be careful not to get them wet.) Most of the coins my dad gives to me, but I also look for neat coins in my pocket change.

Coins were originally used in ancient Greece and Rome as a way to buy things, but they were also used to help celebrate important events like the Olympics. Because the Greek and Roman empires were huge, the use of coins came to many other countries. You can buy some ancient Greek and Roman coins that are thousands of years old for low prices. Ancient coins are collected just like coins made today.

Coins from shipwrecks and treasures are really awesome. Imagine finding old, gold coins in *perfect* condition at the bottom of the ocean! The S.S. *Central America,* which sank in 1857 during a violent hurricane, produced gold coins valued at more than a hundred million dollars, including one gold block that weighed eighty pounds.

Collecting coins from different countries is my favorite way to collect them. I have coins from almost *every* major country in the world! Some of these I got from friends and family members who were in other countries and brought some coins back for me. Some I bought at coin shows when I was with my dad. While he's looking for coins that he likes, I search for stuff that I like or don't have. But you don't just have to collect *coins*. You can also collect foreign bills ranging in value from one dollar to a thousand dollars!

One of my books is a Lincoln cents (penny) book. Did you know that in 1943 copper was needed for World War II so pennies were made of steel? You won't find any of these pennies in your change, but your parents or grandparents might have some, or you can usually find them at coin shows.

My other book is any random coins I find or Dad gives me that I like. I like soccer. So, I have an Olympics commemorative soccer coin from 1996 (girls' soccer). Some of my other favorites are silver dollars, Mercury dimes, and Statehood Quarters.

Statehood Quarters are a good place to start collecting these days. Collecting these coins is my second favorite way to collect. I enjoy collecting Statehood Quarters because it's fun to search for them in your change, and you can also find them at stores and banks (for the same amount they're worth, like trading). When my family went on vacation to the shore, I went food shopping with Dad, and we received some new quarters in our change. We asked at the front if any rolls of quarters were available, and we were able to buy a roll of the new Georgia quarters for the face value.

One of the nice things about the new Statehood Quarters is that each state will have a unique design for the reverse. As you may already know, only five Statehood Quarters will come out each year for a ten-year period, and they will be released in the order the state became part of the United States. For the year 1999, the states were Delaware, Pennsylvania, New Jersey, Connecticut, and Georgia. For my tenth birthday, Dad gave me a set of proof quarters that contained one of each of the five Statehood Quarters for 1999.

I don't have as much interest in coin shows as Dad does, but I do like them. He knows lots of people at coin shows and likes talking to them and looking at coins. Some coins at shows are pretty expensive, but there are a lot of less expensive coins that I can afford for my sets. Most coin dealers are very helpful, but sometimes they are busy. Don't be afraid to ask a question, but remember to be patient and polite. My dad's favorite type of coin to collect are coins with errors. Once in a while he forgets and thinks they're my favorite, too!

Sometimes at coin shows, I get to see other types of collectibles. At a recent show, there were two tables with Pokemon cards. (I'm not crazy about Pokemon cards, but I do collect some.)

Coin collecting is called "The World's Oldest Hobby," and it probably is. I think all kids can collect coins if they want to. It's easy!

The Kid's Guide to Collecting Statehood Quarters

Hunting for the New and Old
by Melissa Boccuti (age 11)

I guess the first coins I ever received were in a proof set. They were dated 1989. I don't remember getting this set because that was when I was born. My dad got it for me. I was a coin collector then, and I didn't even know it. My dad is a part-time coin dealer, so I have been around them all my life. When I was younger, I used to go with him to the coin shops in our area. I would call them the money stores.

I can remember three shows that he would go to all the time. I would sit there as he looked at all the coins. He would show me some of the neater ones now and then. This is how I learned. There were coins I had never even seen. I was used to the coins we all see now, such as the Lincolns, Jeffersons . . . and so on. I knew what was out there from school and how much each was worth. But now I was seeing coins that were still a penny, nickel, dime, and quarter, but they didn't look anything like I had ever seen before! I knew that each coin had a date on it from the year it was made. That's called the mintage year. I was seeing coins that were *very old,* made back in the early 1900s and even older ones from the 1800s. I would think they had to be pretty expensive because they were so old. Some were, but as it turned out, a lot were not.

The dealers my dad and I would visit sometimes gave me old coins. And when I got home, I would ask my dad how much it was worth. As it turned out, the Indian cent in good condition, dated 1890, was only worth about one dollar. As I grew older, I started collecting pennies. I got a Whitman folder 1959 to present and would look for the coins I needed to fill the holes in it. Some of them were easy to find, and some I could not find at all. The mintmarked coins were the hardest to find. The D (Denver) and S (San Francisco) coins were made on the West Coast, and I live on the East Coast. So most of the coins I would look at were P mints (Philadelphia Mint). I would look at all the pennies I could find just to fill a hole in my book. I still need a few more coins in the book to fill it all the way up, but that's what makes it fun. Each year, when the new pennies come out, my dad and I have a contest to see who can find the first coin dated for that year. I usually win. I received my first magnifier when I was six, and it really made the coins easy to see. I still have it and use it all the time.

My dad sets up his coin cases for at least three coin shows a month. My mom and I go to two of them. I remember the first one I went to. It was a big room with, I guess, thirty to forty dealers in it. All of them had tables with showcases and lamps and lots and lots of all kinds of coins. I was a little scared because I didn't know anyone and most of the people there were adults. I stayed at my dad's table and just looked around. A few times my dad asked if I would watch his table while he went to look at another dealer's coins. It was neat to be there as people came to look at what was in my dad's showcase.

As time went on, I started to wander around the room and see what was out there. So many coins. Some dealers have boxes of lower priced coins, and some just have the really good stuff. That means more money. I found out that some dealers like the kids and will answer questions. They'll let me look through their boxes for coins that I need for my collection.

Most people walking around the room have a list of coins that they are looking for. They call that the want list. When I go to coin shows now, I bring a list, but sometimes I bring one of my folders and try to get the coins to fill in the holes. If a dealer is busy with someone, I don't interrupt him. I'll wait or move on to a dealer who is not as busy. Then I ask him if he has any pennies or Walkers. I really like the Walking Liberty half dollars. Sometimes I will show the dealer my book and ask if he has any coins that I need. Being a kid, I don't have a lot of money to spend on them, and some of the dealers don't carry the lower grade stuff that I need. Some dealers do, though, and I have been lucky to find some coins that I need. There is nothing like getting a coin and filling a hole in the book. One less to go, I say with a smile.

I have a *Red Book* that has all the coin pictures in it and the prices. As I said earlier, I like the Walkers. They have a nice picture of a lady (Miss Liberty) on the front and an eagle on the back. Some of the coins are expensive, but most of them I can even afford. I have a 1916, which was the first year they made them, and a 1947, which was the last year. I also have a lot of the dates and mintmarks in between. I found that the dealers that have the lower grade coins remember me when I see them show after show. They're nice and always ask how I am doing with my collection. Most dealers know me by name now because I go there so often.

I have noticed that there are a lot more kids coming to the show in the past few years. I think with the new state quarters coming out, there will be even more. Like all kids, I have collected other things. I was into Beanie Babies and Pokemon cards, but they seemed to die out after a short time. They were neat to collect and are the same as coins in that I tried to get a full set. No one seems to care about them now. I guess you could call them a fad.

My dad tells me coin collecting has been around for a long time and that there will always be collectors of coins. With the new quarters, I can see this as really being something that a kid can collect. It will take ten years to get them in the change you get. A lot of the dealers at the shows carry the new quarters and the folders and maps to put them in. I have a full set so far. I couldn't find a few of the D mintmarks so I bought them at one of the shows. They're not expensive, around fifty cents for each, but they are in uncirculated condition.

The coin shows are a great place to see some really cool coins. You won't believe how many coins there are! Things like half cents and a half of a penny? Yep, they made them and other weird coins like three-cent coins and twenty-cent coins. I don't have any of them, but they sure are cool. There are even gold coins at the shows, small ones to big ones. Nope, don't have any of them yet either, but someday I will. I want to finish my Walker set and then move on to maybe the Buffalo nickels. That coin has an Indian and a buffalo on it. Most of the dates for those are cheap. In the *Red Book,* there are a lot of prices under a dollar each in the lower grades.

My favorite coin is the 3-legged Buffalo nickel. Sometimes I see a boy who goes to school with me at these shows. He and his dad collect coins, too. We talk about the coins we have. Some of the kids in school are collecting the new quarters, too. Maybe I'll see them at the show one day. Collecting coins has been fun for me, and someday I hope to get a full collection of the Lincoln cents. They started in 1909. I get some coins for Christmas each year, mostly the ones I can't afford on my own right now. There are always a few that I put on my list each year. If you collect coins or are thinking about starting, I hope you have as much fun as I do at the coin shows. Give it a try and see. Which coins will you collect?

Introduction

Coin collecting is one of the oldest hobbies in the world. People have been collecting coins since coins were first created about 2,700 years ago. Today, in almost every country, people of all ages enjoy collecting coins. Here in the United States, there are about 5 million people who collect coins.

If you like to save coins from your pocket change, coins from around the world, or have been given coins from a relative, you are on your way to enjoying this hobby. There is no right or wrong way to collect coins. All you need to do is begin by collecting what you like best.

Some people collect coins from different countries to show where they have been or to show where they would like to go. Other people collect coins because they like the image (picture) on the coin.

Putting together a coin collection can be fun and challenging. Coins come in many different shapes and sizes, including round, square, and even triangles. They are also made of different metals, including gold, silver, and copper.

Coins are made in many different shapes and sizes, and of many different metals.

Coins can also teach us about the history of a country at the time the coin was made. The images on most coins are of famous people or important events.

This coin, minted by the Roman Empire, shows a portrait of Julius Caesar.

The U.S. Eisenhower dollar shows President Dwight Eisenhower and a picture representing the moon landing.

Imagine holding a coin from the time of the American Civil War in the 1860s, or the Revolutionary War around 1776, or the time of Columbus in 1492. It is amazing that a little coin could have traveled through all that time. Think of how many different people may have held that coin; maybe a president, a king, a queen, or a famous athlete.

Coin collecting is a great hobby. It's also a good way to meet new friends who enjoy collecting and share what you have learned or found. There are coin shows, stores, clubs, chat sites on the Internet, and other ways to view coins or meet people who enjoy collecting. Sometimes there is a chance to make money in this hobby, but when you are first beginning, collect coins because you enjoy them. Have fun!

Basics of Coins and Money

Parts of a Coin

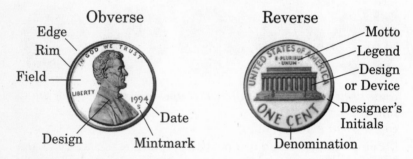

Obverse — Edge, Rim, Field, Design, Date, Mintmark

Reverse — Motto, Legend, Design or Device, Designer's Initials, Denomination

Obverse: Front of the coin.
Reverse: Back of the coin.
Date: The year the coin was struck.
Mintmark: Tells us at which Mint a coin was struck. For example: P stands for Philadelphia, D for Denver, and S for San Francisco.
Design: The main image on the coin. For example, on the Lincoln cent, the main image on the obverse would be the image of President Lincoln. On the reverse, it would be the Lincoln Memorial.
Device: Same as the main design on the coin.
Legend: The words "UNITED STATES OF AMERICA," which are required to be on all coins struck at the United States Mint.

The Kid's Guide to Collecting Statehood Quarters

Motto: The words "E PLURIBUS UNUM," which are required to be on all coins today. This is Latin for "ONE OUT OF MANY."
Rim: This is the outer raised portion of the coin.
Edge: The side of the coin.
Field: The flat surface of the coin.
Designer's Initials: Initials of the person who created the design.
Denomination: The value assigned to the coin. Also known as the face value and the legal tender.

The government of a country is in charge of the money used there. The United States government decides what *legal tender* is used here in the United States. Legal tender is coin or paper money.

The value of money is also known as the *face value*, or *denomination*. This tells us how much a coin or paper money is worth. For example, one dollar is worth a hundred cents.

The value of the metal used in making the coin is called the *intrinsic value*. Often, the intrinsic value and the face value of a coin are very different. For example, the intrinsic value of the metal in the Washington quarter is about three cents, but the face value is twenty-five cents. For the American Eagle fifty-dollar gold piece, the intrinsic value is about $325, but the face value is $50. This is because gold is very valuable.

Money is made at a *mint*. Today, in the United States, coins and paper money are made at the United States Mint in Philadelphia and two branch mints, Denver and San Francisco, but several other branch mints were also used in the past. To tell which mint a coin was made (struck) at, a *mintmark* is placed on the coins. The following mintmarks were used for the eight United States mints where coins have been minted: "C" for Charlotte, "CC" for Carson City, "D" for Dahlonega, "D" for Denver, "O" for New Orleans, "P" for Philadelphia, "S" for San Francisco, and "W" for West Point. Try looking for the mintmark on coins you find. Coins struck at the Philadelphia Mint are mainly found on the East Coast while those struck at Denver are usually found on the West Coast, but over time the coins will mix.

Today, P and D mintmarks are found on coins in circulation.

There are different types of money made at the mint. *Business strikes* are coins that will be used by the public to buy and sell things. Each year billions of these coins are made for general use. Each coin is struck once in the coining press. Then the coins are dumped into bins with millions of others of the same denomination. The coins are sent out to banks so we can use them to buy the items we want.

Some coins are made especially for collectors. These coins are sold as *mint sets*. These sets contain one of each denomination from each mint where the coin was produced. So if the cent, nickel, dime, quarter, and half dollar are being struck at both the Philadelphia and Denver mints for a year, the mint set would contain 10 coins, one of each denomination from each mint. These coins are struck once like business strikes from normal dies, but after they are struck, they are placed into the sets. They are not dumped into bins where they would come in contact with other coins.

A mint set

Proof coins are also made for collectors. The same design is used for business strikes and proofs for each denomination, but proofs are made from special dies that are highly polished to give the coins mirrorlike surfaces. Proof coins are struck twice to make the design really sharp. After each coin is struck it is placed by hand into a set, so there are no *bag marks,* which occur when coins are placed with other coins and bang into each other, causing marks and nicks. Today, proof coins are only struck at the San Francisco Mint.

Proof coins are sold in sets that you can buy from the Mint or coin dealers. Each proof set contains one of each denomination that is made at the Mint. Each coin in a regular proof set is made of the same metal as the business strike. A special *silver proof set* is also made in which the dime, quarter, and half dollar are made of silver instead of the normal clad-copper nickel.

Commemorative coins are made to honor a person or special event. These coins are made in limited numbers and not made for regular circulation. Sometimes commemorative coins are created to help pay for monuments or special events. *Prestige sets* are proof sets that contain commemorative coins struck in that year.

This commemorative coin from 1996 honors the U.S. Women's Olympic Soccer Team.

Handling and Examining Coins

It is very important to always handle coins with care. If coins are handled incorrectly, they can be ruined forever. A few simple rules will help keep your coins in the best condition.

1. Touch your coins as little as possible. If you have to pick up your coin, hold it only by the edges. **Never touch the front (obverse) or back (reverse) of the coin.** Even putting your coin in the palm of your hand can damage a coin. Our skin has oil, plus if there is any dirt on your hands, it can get on the coin. Try to wash your hands before handling coins and make sure they are dry. You could also wear cotton gloves to be completely safe.

2. Do not eat or drink while examining your coins. If you have to cough or sneeze, put the coin down and turn your head. Try not to talk or breathe on the coin, because even vapor can affect the surface of the coin.

3. If you want to hold the coin to examine it, hold the coin between your thumb and index finger. Make sure you keep a soft mat on the table under the coin in case it falls. The condition of a coin has a great deal to do with its value. If a coin is

dented, scratched, tarnished, or has fingerprints on it, it will be far less valuable.

4. Do not attempt to clean a coin. If a coin shows signs of cleaning, it is worth far less.

Examine your coins in good, strong light. Hold the coin about two to three feet from the light, then tilt the coin at an angle so that the light reflects from the coin's surface to your eye. Tilt and turn the coin so that different parts of the coin can be observed.

Always hold a coin by its edges when examining it.

It is important to examine all parts of the coin. The value of the coin mainly depends on the condition of the coin. For circulated coins, the amount of wear is the most important part in determining condition. For mint-state coins or coins that have no signs of wear from circulation, the number of marks, scratches, contact marks, nicks, color, and eye appeal are all important. A small difference in the condition of the coin can have a big difference in its value.

To look at a coin very closely, use a magnifying glass. There are

A magnifying glass will help you see the smallest parts of your coins.

many different types of magnifying glasses. They come in different shapes and different power levels. Some have lights attached to them. One of the most popular is the 5X packette, which is made by Bausch & Lomb. When buying a magnifying glass, bring a coin with you and examine it through different glasses to see which you like the best.

Grading Coins

Coin grading is an important part of coin collecting. It is the most important thing that you need to learn if you really want to collect coins. The grade of a coin has to do with how much wear or circulation the coin has received. More use leads to the coin's design becoming more worn, which affects the coin's condition and value.

There are many books that can help you learn how to grade coins. Two of the standard books are: *Photograde* and *Official ANA Grading Standards for United States Coins*. These books are helpful tools, but the best way to learn how to grade coins is to examine various graded coins and see the differences on the coin.

The grade of a coin is one of the most important factors in establishing its value. Coins made for circulation are given a grade from 0 through 70, with 70 being perfect condition. Some of the general terms and standards to describe the grade of a coin are given on page 8. Lincoln cents are shown as an example for each grade.

In grading, the *design* of the coin means the main image. On the Lincoln penny, the obverse *design* is the image of President Lincoln. The *lettering* or *legend* is usually the lettering around the rim of the coin. The *date* is the date the coin was struck, which is usually seen at the bottom of the front of the coin. The *highest point* on the coin is the part of the design that is raised the highest above the surface of the coin and usually will begin to wear first.

About Good (AG-3): Very heavily worn. Design worn smooth, but the general outline is still visible. Most of letters around the rim are only partially visible. The date is worn but visible, allowing you to tell which year the coin was struck.

Good (G-4): Heavily worn. Most of the design is worn flat, but major parts of the design are visible. Letters around rim are worn but mostly visible. Date is fully visible.

Very Good (VG-8): Well worn. Major features of design flat, but visible. Letters around rim are clear.

Fine (F-12): Moderate to considerable wear. Entire design is bold, with some higher points visible.

Very Fine (VF-20): Moderate wear on high points of design. Major details are clear.

Extremely Fine (EF-40): Only slight wear. Major features of design are sharp and well defined.

About Uncirculated (AU-50): Traces of light wear seen on most of the highest points of the design.

Mint-state coins show no signs of wear. The grade of a mint-state coin is based on the coin's luster, number of bag marks, scuff marks, location of marks, color of the coin, and eye appeal.

MS-60: Many possible large bag marks, *hairlines,* or scuff marks throughout. Possible rim nicks. Poor eye appeal. Surfaces may be dull or spotted. Dull luster.

MS-63: Only a few scattered large bag marks in prime areas, numerous small bag marks. A few small scattered patches of hairlines in secondary areas. Several possible scuff marks in fields and on the design. Attractive eye appeal. Surfaces have some original color. Luster may be slightly impaired.

MS-65: One or two large contact marks in prime areas or a few small contact marks. One or two small patches of hairlines. A few scuff marks on high points of design. Very pleasing eye appeal. Surfaces have full original color or tone. Attractive average luster throughout.

MS-70: Perfect coin. Outstanding eye appeal. Surfaces bright with lustrous original color. Very attractive, blazing luster.

The more coins you study, the better you will be at telling what grade a coin is. Study as many coins as you can and compare coins to see differences. Always remember the grade of a coin is based on personal opinion. If someone tells you it is one grade and you disagree, then you should not buy the coin. Each person grades differently and you must learn to trust your own experience by practicing and examining many different coins.

Buying Coins

The best way to start a collection is to find coins in circulation, but sometimes the coins you need to complete your collection can't be found in your change. Then you may want to consider buying them.

There are many places to buy coins and accessories. You can try your local coin dealer or a coin show. If there aren't any nearby, try mail order.

If you are considering buying coins, you should first plan with your parents how much you are going to spend and think about what you want. What grades, quality, and colors do you like best? Consider the strength of a coin's *strike* and how some coins can change color over time. After you pick a series that you want to collect, buy a book on the series, which will tell you what to look for in grading, color, and availability.

Look around at coin shows and see what you like. Do not buy the first coin you see that you need. It is best to shop around, find the coin you want, and find the best price. Often, coin dealers mark the price of the coin on their holders, but many will come down in price if you ask them nicely what their best price would be for the coin.

Always remember that when you are buying coins, be careful if someone wants to sell you a coin for a lot less than it's worth. There may be something wrong with the coin.

Storing Coins

It's important to store your coins properly so they do not become damaged. You should not place your coins in a bag all together or throw them in your drawer, because the coins can bang against each other and they will become nicked and scratched.

There are many different ways to store your coins to keep them protected. The best way for you depends on what you collect and what your goals are.

If you want to collect all the coins of a series, the most affordable way is to use coin folders. These folders provide a space for each coin made for general use, including all dates and mint-marks. Only one side of the coin can be seen. With coin folders, there is no plastic protection for the front and back of the coin. When you put coins into the folder's holes, you may have to use a little muscle, as the holes are made small so the coins will not fall out. Put the top of the coin in first, then the bottom. Coin folders can be bought for almost any United States coin series.

A Jefferson nickels coin folder

If you are collecting a complete set of each date and mintmark for a single series and you want very good protection for your coins, coin albums are the best choice, though they are a little more expensive than folders. Coin albums are books in which both sides of the coins can be viewed. There is a removable plastic slide to protect both sides of the coin. Albums are probably the best and safest way to store your coins.

When removing or inserting coins from albums, make sure you use a glove, cloth, or piece of plastic so that you do not damage the coin. Do not push on the front or back of the coin with your bare finger. First, holding the coins by the edge between your thumb and index finger, place the coin over the place you are going to put it in the album.

Second, place either a cardboard holder or cloth over the coin. With the thumb and index finger, push down on the rim of the coin. Make sure the coin is even, not one side down farther than the other, so that air pockets do not form around the coin.

Inserting a coin into an album.

If you like to collect all types of coins and keep them together, the easiest way to store your coins is in 2" by 2" cardboard holders with plastic windows. There are different sizes for different size coins.

A cardboard holder.

To insert a coin, first choose a holder where the window is the same size as the coin. Lay the holder flat, place the coin on top in the middle, fold over the holder, and staple it shut. When you staple, it is best to staple around all four sides. Make sure you do not accidentally staple your coin. You can write notes on the cardboard holders to remind yourself about each coin, for example, when you bought it, how much you paid, or anything special that you like about the coin.

Once you have your coins in these holders, you can put the coins in boxes or in vinyl pages where you can put up to twenty coins in a page. These pages fit into a three-ring binder and allow you to enjoy your coins in a book format.

A three-ring binder is another way to store your coins.

Another way of storing single coins is in *flips*. Flips are clear plastic envelopes with two pockets. These can be used to display two coins, or a single coin with a description of the coin or any other information. Some are made of vinyl, which is soft and easy to use, but not recommended for long-term storage because the oil in the vinyl can cause damage to the coins over time. Other flips are made of a different material that is more expensive. These flips are stiffer, and oil is removed from the vinyl to avoid damage to your coins during long-term storage. Make sure you ask when you buy flips if they are safe for long-term storage. You can also store your coins in inexpensive paper envelopes and write any notes on the envelope.

The problem with a cardboard holder, flip, or paper holder is that the coin can still be damaged if it is dropped or banged into other coins. To avoid this, you can use hard plastic holders. With hard plastic holders you get to see both sides of the coin, the coin is protected, and you can use stickers to put notes on the holders.

A plastic holder like this one will protect your coin from many types of damage.

Some plastic holders hold all denominations for a given year. This would be useful if you want to store one of each proof coin for a year.

Another way to store coins is in tubes, which are clear rolls for coins. These are great for extra coins that are not very expensive. Tubes allow you to store many of your coins together.

Whichever way you choose to store your coins, make sure they are stored in a safe place. They should not be near heat or moisture or a place where the temperature changes a lot. A desk or dresser drawer should be fine as long as it is not too close to a window or radiator.

How to Start a Coin Collection

There are many different ways to collect coins. You could collect one of each of the Statehood Quarters. You could collect one of each denomination from the year you were born. If you really like one denomination—such as Lincoln cents—you could collect one of each date the coin was made, or even one of each date and mintmark that the coin was made.

The easiest and best way to start collecting is to collect a series that is currently being made by the Mint. These coins can be found in your pocket change. There are five different denominations currently being struck at the United States Mint. They are the Lincoln cent, Jefferson nickel, Roosevelt dime, Fifty States quarter, and Kennedy half dollar. These series are each covered in detail later in this book. Collecting a current series is a fun and inexpensive way to start, since you will not have to pay extra for the coins and you should be able to find them in your change.

Another easy way to start a collection is to start on a recent series that was only made for a few years. The Susan B. Anthony dollar was only struck from 1979 to 1981 and in 1999. The Eisenhower dollar was only struck from 1971 to 1978. Coins from these series can be bought cheaply at coin shows or shops. Your parents or grandparents might also have some.

Die varieties and error coins can be fun to collect. You can learn more about these coins later in this book.

One way to add to the fun of collecting is to join a club. There are many local, regional, and national clubs for collectors, and many have special programs for young coin collectors, also known as Young Numismatists or YNs. The **American Numismatic Association** (ANA) is the world's largest coin club and sponsors many events and activities for young collectors, including The World's Fair of Money, which is the largest coin show in America, ANA National Coin Week, and the ANA YN Treasure Trivia Game. The ANA can also tell you about the clubs and activities in your area.

To learn more about all the ANA has to offer, check out their Web site at www.money.org, call toll-free at 1-800-367-9723, or write to them at The American Numismatic Association, 818 North Cascade Avenue, Colorado Springs, CO 80903-3279. ANA junior membership costs $11.00 a year and includes a subscription to the monthly magazine *The Numismatist* and *First Strike,* a special twice-a-year section for YNs. There is an application for ANA membership at the back of this book.

Statehood Quarters

One of the newest and most exciting ways to start collecting coins has just begun, a program in which each of the fifty states will design the back of a quarter dollar. Starting in 1999, five new quarters will be struck each year for ten years, with quarters being issued in the order the states joined the Union. Normal Washington quarters will not be struck during these ten years.

Though George Washington will still be on the front, there are some changes to the front of these new quarters. One of the most interesting is that the date will be found on the back of the coin. Only a few coins ever struck at the United States Mint have had the date on the back. Another change is that QUARTER DOLLAR and UNITED STATES OF AMERICA, which are on the back of the Washington quarters, are now on the front of these new quarters. E PLURIBUS UNUM is on the reverse of the new quarters.

Can you find all the changes made to the front of the new Statehood Quarters?

The back of each coin will have the new designs for each state. Many states are having contests to pick the new design, so if you have artistic talent and your state hasn't already chosen a design, you might want to give it a try. You can print out an outline in which to draw your design from the U.S. Mint Web site at www.usmint.gov.

Like normal Washington quarters, the new Statehood Quarters are made of a metal called *clad coinage*. The top layer is made of copper and nickel, while the inside is made of copper. The Mint will also be making special proof sets of the new quarters in which silver will be used. These sets will be available through the Mint and coin dealers.

Starting a collection of Statehood Quarters is easy. The best and most exciting way is to look for these quarters in your pocket change. You can also get uncirculated coins from any bank. I would recommend finding the coins yourself because it is more fun.

The easiest way to start collecting these quarters is to find one of each state quarter. Or you could try for the P and D mintmarks of each state quarter. These will probably be the most common ways to collect since both mintmarks are available in regular change. Look to see which mintmark you see most often. P coins are more often found on the East Coast, while D coins are mostly found on the West Coast. If you have friends or family in another part of the country, you might want to trade mintmarks by mail!

Once you decide whether you want to collect just one of each of the fifty state quarters or one each of the P and D mintmarks, you will need a place to store them. In addition to the ways we talked about in the Storing Coins chapter, there are many different special books, boards, and other ways to save Statehood Quarters. There are map boards that you can hang on your wall and books and cases for storing these fun coins.

One of the nicest ways to collect just the fifty states is with a map with individual cutouts for each state. You can hang this on your wall and keep track of the coins you have and those you need. You will have to be careful with these, because there is nothing covering the coins.

Map boards can be a fun way to store your collection of Statehood Quarters.

Another great way to hold a collection of one of each state is with a special Statehood Collector's Folder. This is a colorful folder with plastic cutouts to hold each coin and a booklet of fun state facts and information on coin collecting.

The United States Mint has started a Web site for kids that has lots of information about the Statehood Quarters Program. The Web address is http://www.usmint.gov. Follow the directions to the kids h.i.p. pocket change ™ section. You will find informa-

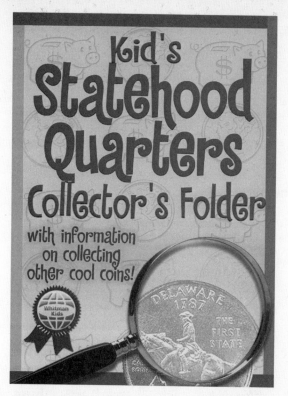

The Kid's Statehood Quarters Collector's Folder *is another great way to safely store your collection.*

tion here about each state quarter and a schedule of when each coin will be available.

The following page is a list of all fifty states in the order in which they became part of the United States. This is the order in which the state quarter will be issued. Also listed is the state's capital, and the year it came into the United States. Then, read on for more information about each state and its coin.

State	Capital	Statehood	State	Capital	Statehood
Delaware	Dover	1787	Michigan	Lansing	1837
Pennsylvania	Harrisburg	1787	Florida	Tallahassee	1845
New Jersey	Trenton	1787	Texas	Austin	1845
Georgia	Atlanta	1788	Iowa	Des Moines	1846
Connecticut	Hartford	1788	Wisconsin	Madison	1848
Massachusetts	Boston	1788	California	Sacramento	1850
Maryland	Annapolis	1788	Minnesota	St. Paul	1858
South Carolina	Columbia	1788	Oregon	Salem	1859
New Hampshire	Concord	1788	Kansas	Topeka	1861
Virginia	Richmond	1788	West Virginia	Charleston	1863
New York	Albany	1788	Nevada	Carson City	1864
North Carolina	Raleigh	1789	Nebraska	Lincoln	1867
Rhode Island	Providence	1790	Colorado	Denver	1876
Vermont	Montpelier	1791	North Dakota	Bismarck	1889
Kentucky	Frankfort	1792	South Dakota	Pierre	1889
Tennessee	Nashville	1796	Montana	Helena	1889
Ohio	Columbus	1803	Washington	Olympia	1889
Louisiana	Baton Rouge	1812	Idaho	Boise	1890
Indiana	Indianapolis	1816	Wyoming	Cheyenne	1890
Mississippi	Jackson	1817	Utah	Salt Lake City	1896
Illinois	Springfield	1818	Oklahoma	Oklahoma City	1907
Alabama	Montgomery	1819	New Mexico	Santa Fe	1912
Maine	Augusta	1820	Arizona	Phoenix	1912
Missouri	Jefferson City	1821	Alaska	Juneau	1959
Arkansas	Little Rock	1836	Hawaii	Honolulu	1959

The Kid's Guide to Collecting Statehood Quarters

DELAWARE

NICKNAME: **THE FIRST STATE** • STATE FLOWER: **PEACH BLOSSOM** • STATE BIRD: **BLUE HEN CHICKEN**

The state of Delaware was the first of the thirteen original colonies to sign the Constitution on December 7, 1787. This state and the bay and river on its eastern side were named for Lord De La Warr.

•Dover

The reverse of this coin shows Caesar Rodney on horseback. Caesar Rodney was a famous patriot from the state of Delaware who served as a general in the Revolutionary War and was one of the signers of the Declaration of Independence. He was also governor of the state of Delaware and a justice on Delaware's Supreme Court.

In the spring of 1776, the Continental Congress was meeting to discuss breaking away from British rule over the colonies. On July 2, 1776, the Congress was going to take a vote. At that time, there were two representatives from Delaware: Tom McKean, who favored independence and George Reed, who did not. Rodney made an eighty-mile ride on horseback and arrived at Independence Hall with just minutes to spare to cast his vote for independence and break the Delaware tie. This historic ride on horseback was voted by Delawareans to represent their state.

PENNSYLVANIA

NICKNAME: **KEYSTONE STATE** • STATE FLOWER: **MOUNTAIN LAUREL** • STATE BIRD: **RUFFED GROUSE**

Founded by William Penn in 1681, the state was originally supposed to be named "Sylvania," which means woodlands. King Charles II of England suggested adding "Penn" in honor of William Penn's father, a great admiral. William Penn's "Great Law" protected life, liberty, and property through a jury trial. He also wrote the Charter of Privileges in 1701.

Harrisburg

Philadelphia, Pennsylvania, hosted some of our country's most important founding conventions. The city hosted the Continental Congress in 1776, where the Declaration of Independence was signed, and the Federal Constitutional Convention in 1787, where the Constitution of the United States was written. Philadelphia was also the second capital of the United States.

The reverse of the Pennsylvania state quarter shows an allegorical female figure named Commonwealth. The state's motto, "VIRTUE, LIBERTY, and INDEPENDENCE" is to the right of the statue, and an outline of the state of Pennsylvania is in the background.

NEW JERSEY

NICKNAME: **GARDEN STATE** • STATE FLOWER: **PURPLE VIOLET** • STATE BIRD: **EASTERN GOLDFINCH**

New Jersey was settled by the Dutch in the early seventeenth century. Named after England's Isle of Jersey, the land was then given in 1664 by the Duke of York to John Berkeley and Sir George Cartaret. Located between New York and Philadelphia, the two major cities of the colonies, many historic battles were fought in New Jersey during the American Revolution, including the one before General George Washington crossed the Delaware River late on Christmas night. He led the army to a great victory the next day. Washington's historic crossing was chosen as the subject of the New Jersey state quarter, and the design is based on the 1851 painting by Emmanuel Leutze. The words "Crossroads of the Revolution" are printed under the design.

New Jersey was the third state to join the Union, signing the Constitution on December 18, 1787. Before this, from June 30 to November 4, 1783, Princeton served as a temporary national capital, as did Trenton from November 1 to December 24, 1784. In the twentieth century, Thomas

The Kid's Guide to Collecting Statehood Quarters

Edison invented the light bulb and many other inventions such as the alkaline storage battery and the phonograph at his laboratory in New Jersey.

GEORGIA

NICKNAME: **EMPIRE STATE OF THE SOUTH** • STATE FLOWER: **CHEROKEE ROSE** • STATE BIRD: **BROWN THRASHER**

Georgia was first inhabited by Cherokee and Creek Native Americans. In 1540, it was claimed by Hernando de Soto for Spain. In 1733, James E. Oglethorpe and a group of about 120 followers built a settlement on the Savannah River around Yamacraw Bluff.

Though Georgia is sometimes called the "Peach State," after its most famous fruit, its official nickname is "The Empire State of the South." Georgia is named after King George II of England, who in 1732 granted Oglethorpe the charter to settle a colony. The design of Georgia's state quarter is of a peach inside the outline of the state of Georgia. A banner reading the state's motto, "Wisdom, Justice, Moderation," is draped on the outside with oak sprigs.

Georgia has been the home of many famous Americans. Eli Whitney invented the cotton gin in 1793, which separated cotton seeds from the fiber and revolutionized the cotton industry. Civil rights leader Dr. Martin Luther King, Jr., was also born in Georgia. Georgia was the fourth state to sign the Constitution.

CONNECTICUT

NICKNAME: **CONSTITUTION STATE** • STATE FLOWER: **MOUNTAIN LAUREL** • STATE BIRD: **AMERICAN ROBIN**

Connecticut was first claimed by a Dutch explorer, Adrian Block, in 1614, but Block and his followers were soon driven out by English settlers who migrated west from Massachusetts. In 1639, settlers from the towns of Wethersfield, Windsor, and Hartford formed their own laws—the Fundamental Orders of Connecticut. This document gave people the right to elect government officials. In 1662, Governor John Winthrop obtained a royal charter from England, making Connecticut an official independent colony.

The design of this state quarter shows a white oak with the words "The Charter Oak" to the left. There is a great story behind this design.

The 1662 British charter gave Connecticut the right to govern itself and established the borders of the state, but on October 31, 1687, Sir Edmund Andros, a British representative of King James II, tried to take the charter of Connecticut back.

At a meeting between Sir Andros and representatives of Connecticut, while the charter sat on a table between the two sides, the candles mysteriously went out. When they were relit, the charter was missing. The charter had been taken by Captain Joseph Wadsworth, who hid it in a white oak on the property of the Wyllys family. Since the British could not take the charter back, Captain Wadsworth had saved Connecticut from returning to British rule. Connecticut signed the Constitution on January 9, 1788.

MASSACHUSETTS

NICKNAME: **BAY STATE** • STATE FLOWER: **MAYFLOWER** • STATE BIRD: **CHICKADEE**

On February 6, 1788, Massachusetts became the sixth state to join the Union. The design on this coin includes the words "The Bay State," which is the state's nickname, an outline of the state with a star showing its capital in Boston, and a figure of a Minuteman.

The Minuteman figure represents volunteer soldiers who fought the British during the Revolutionary War. Their name came from the idea that they would be ready in a minute to fight for the freedom of this country.

Massachusetts gets its name from an Algonquian word meaning "place of big hills." The motto "The Bay State" comes from Massachusetts Bay, the area where the pilgrims first settled when the *Mayflower* landed at Plymouth Rock in 1620.

Massachusetts is rich in history. The Boston Tea Party, the battle of Bunker Hill, "The Shot Heard Around The World," and Paul Revere are all represented by the patriotic Minuteman symbol.

MARYLAND

NICKNAME: **OLD LINE STATE** • STATE FLOWER: **BLACK-EYED SUSAN** • STATE BIRD: **BALTIMORE ORIOLE**

Annapolis

Maryland was the seventh state to join the Union, on April 22, 1788. This state's design features the Maryland State House dome with oak leaf clusters on both sides. The state's motto, "The Old Line State," also appears.

The first European explorer to come here was probably Giovanni da Verrazano, an Italian explorer in the 1500s. In the 1600s, many English settlers came and settled in the Chesapeake Bay area to escape religious oppression and find new jobs. Maryland was named after Queen Maria, the wife of King Charles I of England.

Maryland got its nickname, the Old Line State, during the Revolutionary War when four hundred soldiers fought against ten thousand British soldiers and helped General George Washington's army escape. The soldiers bravely earned Maryland its nickname.

SOUTH CAROLINA

NICKNAME: **THE PALMETTO STATE** • STATE FLOWER: **CAROLINA YELLOW JESSAMINE** • STATE BIRD: **CAROLINA WREN**

Columbia

On May 23, 1788, South Carolina became the eighth state to join the Union. Featured on this quarter are the Carolina wren, a palmetto tree, a yellow jessamine, and the state outline with a star indicating the state capital of Columbia. The state motto, "The Palmetto State," is also printed.

South Carolina was first explored in the sixteenth century by the Spanish and French. They found Native Americans—mainly of the Cherokee and Catabas tribes—living in the region. The first permanent English settlement in South Carolina was established in 1670 near present-day Charleston.

In 1760, Carolina was divided into North and South Carolina. During the Revolutionary War, many battles were fought in this region. South Carolina was the first state to secede from the Union on December 20, 1860, in protest over the restriction of free trade and the calls for stopping slavery. On April 12, 1861, the first shots of the Civil War were fired at Fort Sumter.

NEW HAMPSHIRE

NICKNAME: **GRANITE STATE** • STATE FLOWER: **PURPLE LILAC** • STATE BIRD: **PURPLE FINCH**

Concord

New Hampshire, the most northern of the original thirteen colonies, became the ninth state on June 21, 1788. The main design of this coin is a profile view of a rock formation called The Old Man of the Mountain. The words "Old Man of the Mountain," the state motto "Live Free or Die," and nine stars representing the ninth state are also shown.

New Hampshire was settled in 1623 by Englishmen wanting to establish a fishing colony for Eng-

land. It is known as the Granite State because of
its many granite mountains. One of the most famous mountains is The Old Man of the Mountain,
which is a rock formation that resembles the profile of a man.

At the famous Battle of Bunker Hill in Massachusetts most of the soldiers were from New
Hampshire. New Hampshire Captain John Paul
Jones also had many victories at sea to help the
new colonies win their independence from England.

VIRGINIA

NICKNAME: **MOTHER OF PRESIDENTS** • STATE FLOWER:
AMERICAN DOGWOOD • STATE BIRD: **CARDINAL**

Virginia became the tenth state on June 25, 1788.
Three seventeenth-century ships are the featured
design on this quarter, which commemorates the
quadricentennial of the settlement of Jamestown
(1607–2007). A quadricentennial is a 400th anniversary. This quarter will feature three separate dates: 1788, which represents the state's
entrance into the Union; 1607–2007, which represents the 400th anniversary; and 2000, which is
the date of issue.

Richmond•

Jamestown was the first permanent English
settlement in North America and home to the oldest continuous legislative body in this part of the
world. In June of 1606, King James I chartered
the "Virginia Company" to find a way to the Ori-
ent. Instead, these settlers landed on Jamestown
Island. The new settlers faced many difficulties,
including disease, famine, and Indian attacks.
However, through the leadership of Captain John
Smith, the colony took root and began to prosper
after the marriage of Pocahantas, a native, to set-
tler John Rolfe, bringing peace between the Native Americans and the settlers. The settlement
became a part of the Virginia colony in 1624 and
was the capital of Virginia until 1698.

NEW YORK

NICKNAME: **THE EMPIRE STATE** • STATE FLOWER: **ROSE** • STATE BIRD: **BLUEBIRD**

New York was the eleventh state to join the Union, on July 26, 1788. Originally settled by the Dutch and named New Netherland, in 1664 it became an English colony and was renamed for the Duke of York. New York City was the first capital of the United States, from 1789–90. Today, New York is the largest city in the United States and is the leading center in the country for banking, finance, tourism, broadcasting, and many other things.

New York was the birthplace to several Presidents including Martin Van Buren, Millard Fillmore, Theodore Roosevelt, and Franklin D. Roosevelt. New York is home to several attractions such as Niagara Falls and the Erie Canal. Two famous landmarks, the Statue of Liberty and the Empire State Building, are both in New York City. New York is known as the Empire State, a nickname that came from George Washington when, during a tour of the state's harbors, waterways, and farmlands, he referred to New York as the seat of the New American empire.

NORTH CAROLINA

NICKNAME: **TARHEEL STATE** • STATE FLOWER: **DOGWOOD** • STATE BIRD: **CARDINAL**

Originally named in honor of Charles IX of France and then in honor of Charles I and II of England, North Carolina became the twelvth state on November 21, 1789. Sir Walter Raleigh established the first English colony in the New World at Roanoke Island in 1585. In 1587, a second group of settlers arrived, but both groups disappeared around 1590. These groups of settlers are known as the Lost Colony of Roanoke since they mysteriously disappeared and were never found. North and South Carolina were one colony until they were divided in 1729.

North Carolina is the largest producer of tobacco and textiles and leads in several other industries, including furniture, corn, cotton, peanuts, and vegetables. At Kitty Hawk, on the North Carolina coast, the Wright Brothers made the first successful airplane flight, which lasted for twelve seconds. Cape Hatteras, North Carolina, is home to one of the most famous lighthouses in the country. Three Presidents were born in North Carolina: Andrew Jackson, James Polk, and Andrew Johnson.

RHODE ISLAND

NICKNAME: **THE OCEAN STATE** • STATE FLOWER: **VIOLET**
• STATE BIRD: **RHODE ISLAND RED**

Providence

In 1636, Roger Williams started the colony of Providence after being exiled from Massachusetts because of his religious beliefs. In 1774, Rhode Island became the first state to forbid the slave trade. Rhode Island was also the first colony to declare independence from Great Britain in 1776, but it was the last of the original thirteen to sign the Constitution because it was waiting for the addition of the Bill of Rights. Dutch explorer Adrian Block first named the area "Roodt Eylandt" for the red clay in the area. This was later changed to Rhode Island under English rule.

Rhode Island consists of the mainland and thirty-six islands, which are very popular for vacationing, fishing, and other water activities. Rhode Island is a leading producer of wool, silver, and jewelry. In the nineteenth century, Newport, Rhode Island, was a favorite vacation spot for America's rich and famous.

VERMONT

NICKNAME: **THE GREEN MOUNTAIN STATE** • STATE FLOWER: **RED CLOVER** • STATE BIRD: **HERMIT THRUSH**

On March 4, 1791, Vermont became the four-teenth state to join the Union. The colonies of New York and New Hampshire argued over the possession of this land between Connecticut and the Hudson River for over a hundred years until Great Britain gave the territory to New York in 1761. But the settlers in the region wanted to be independent. Led by Ethan Allan and his "Green Mountain Boys," they supported independence from Great Britain in 1776. In 1777, delegates in a meeting declared it a republic, independent from both New York and New Hampshire. The name Vermont comes from the French for "green mountains"—the French explorer Champlain, who saw Vermont's Green Mountains from a dis-tance, first called them "Verd Mont." The Green Mountains cover most of this beautiful state.

Vermont is the United States' leading producer of maple syrup. Other important industries in-clude tourism, cattle, granite, and marble. Fa-mous people born in Vermont include Presidents Chester Arthur and Calvin Coolidge. This state prides itself on its people's independence.

KENTUCKY

NICKNAME: **THE BLUEGRASS STATE** • STATE FLOWER: **GOLDENROD** • STATE BIRD: **KENTUCKY CARDINAL**

Kentucky became the fifteenth state to join the Union on June 1, 1792. It was the first state west of the Appalachian Mountains. The name Ken-tucky comes from the Indian word meaning "land of tomorrow." Kentucky was first a province of Virginia, becoming a territory in 1790 and then a state in 1792.

Kentucky's nickname is the Bluegrass State due to a type of tall, bluish-green grass found in the region. The state motto is "United We Stand

Divided We Fall." Parts of Kentucky are also known as horse country because some of the world's finest horses are raised and trained there.

Famous Kentuckian Daniel Boone helped blaze the Wilderness Trail through the Cumberland Gap in the Appalachian Mountains. Kentucky is also home to our country's gold depository at Fort Knox. The famous Kentucky Derby is held every May at Churchill Downs in Louisville. Kentucky is the leading producer of coal in the country and is also a major producer of tobacco and horses. Famous people born in Kentucky include President Abraham Lincoln and Confederate President Jefferson Davis—both of the leaders of our divided nation during the Civil War.

TENNESSEE

NICKNAME: **THE VOLUNTEER STATE** • STATE FLOWER: **IRIS** • STATE BIRD: **MOCKINGBIRD**

This sixth state, which joined the Union on June 1, 1796, is nicknamed the Volunteer State. In 1846, over thirty thousand Tennessee men volunteered to help fight the Mexican War. They also helped Andrew Jackson in the Battle of New Orleans. During the Civil War, Tennessee was the last state to secede from the Union and the first to return after the war. The name Tennessee comes from the Cherokee Indians, who first called two villages along the Tennessee River "Tanasi."

Tennessee is famous for country & western music, the capital of which is Nashville, home to the Grand Ole Opry and the Country Music Hall of Fame. Elvis Presley's Memphis home, Graceland, has also become a national shrine visited by millions of people each year. Tennessee is a leading producer of tobacco, wood, chemicals, textiles, and clothing. Frontiersman Davy Crockett was one of many famous people born in Tennessee.

OHIO

NICKNAME: **THE BUCKEYE STATE** • STATE FLOWER: **SCARLET CARNATION** • STATE BIRD: **CARDINAL**

Ohio, the seventeenth state, joined the Union on March 1, 1803. It was the first state formed from the Northwest Territory, and many problems arose there between early settlers and Native Americans. In 1795, a treaty signed by the Indians gave two-thirds of Ohio to the United States. The name Ohio comes from an Iroquois word meaning "beautiful."

Ohio is one of the leading producers of steel, iron, rubber, glass, and machinery. Ohio has been the birthplace of many Presidents, including Ulysses S. Grant, Rutherford Hayes, James Garfield, Benjamin Harrison, William McKinley, William Howard Taft, and Warren Harding. Famous sharpshooter Annie Oakley and astronauts John Glenn and Neil Armstrong were also from this great state. America's first traffic light was installed in Cincinnati way back in 1914. "Hang on Sloopy" is Ohio's official rock song.

LOUISIANA

NICKNAME: **THE PELICAN STATE** • STATE FLOWER: **MAGNOLIA** • STATE BIRD: **BROWN PELICAN**

Louisiana was the eighteenth state to join the Union, on April 30, 1812. The explorer Robert La Salle was the first person to go all the way down the Mississippi River to the delta in 1682. He named the area La Louisianne after Louis XIV of France. Louisiana was part of the Louisiana Purchase. During the War of 1812, it was the site of one of the greatest American victories over Britain. During the Civil War it seceded in 1861 and was readmitted in 1865.

In 1815, President Thomas Jefferson doubled the size of the United States with the Louisiana Purchase from France for $15 million. This included the land between the Mississippi River and the Rocky Mountains and between Canada and the Gulf of Mexico.

New Orleans is a famous tourist attraction, known for Mardi Gras, jazz, and its restaurants. The Superdome is the world's largest enclosed stadium. Louisiana is the only state in the nation that is not divided into counties. It is divided, instead, into "parishes." This state is home to many "Cajun," descendants of a group of settlers called Acadians. The Acadians were driven out of Canada in the 1700s because they refused to pledge allegiance to the King of England.

INDIANA

NICKNAME: **HOOSIER STATE** • STATE FLOWER: **PEONY** • STATE BIRD: **CARDINAL**

Indiana was the nineteenth state to enter the Union, on December 11, 1815. French explorer Robert La Salle first explored the region in 1679. In 1763, after the French and Indian War, Indiana became a British colony. In 1800, Congress created the name Indiana when it created the Indiana Territory out of the Northwest Territory. The name Indiana means "Land of the Indians." Indiana was the center of Indian uprisings until the victory by William Henry Harrison at Tippecanoe in 1811.

Indianapolis

Indiana is famous for the Indianapolis 500 auto race, which is held every Memorial Day at the Indianapolis Motor Speedway. This race, first held on May 30, 1911, was the first long-distance auto race held in the U.S.

MISSISSIPPI

NICKNAME: **MAGNOLIA STATE** • STATE FLOWER:
MAGNOLIA FLOWER • STATE BIRD: **MOCKINGBIRD**

Mississippi became the twentieth state, joining
the Union on December 10, 1817. The state is
named after the Mississippi River, which comes
from a Chippewa word meaning "Father of Wa-
ters." During the Civil War, Mississippi seceded
from the Union on January 9, 1861, and was readmitted after the war on February 23, 1870.

Mississippi is well known for its old plantation
houses and the steam-powered riverboats that
moved goods up and down the river. The main
products from Mississippi include cotton, soybeans, rice, sorghum, and sugarcane. Mississippi
was the site of many civil rights demonstrations
during the 1950s and 1960s.

ILLINOIS

NICKNAME: **LAND OF LINCOLN** • STATE FLOWER: **VIOLET**
• STATE BIRD: **CARDINAL**

Illinois became the twenty-first state to join the
Union, on December 3, 1818. The name Illinois
comes from the French spelling of the Illinois and
Peoria Indian word "ilini," the plural which is
"iliniwok," which means a man or a warrior, or a
member of the Illinois tribe. The French explorer
Robert La Salle, while traveling up the Illinois
River in 1679, chose the name Illinois after the
native Indians who lived along the banks of the
river. In 1865, Illinois was the first state to ratify
the Thirteenth Amendment to the Constitution,
which abolished slavery.

Major industries for Illinois include iron, steel,
grain exchange, and meat packing. Agricultural
products include cattle, corn, hogs, and soybeans.
The world's first skyscraper was built in Chicago
in 1885, and Chicago's Sear's Tower is the tallest
building on the continent of North America.

The Kid's Guide to Collecting Statehood Quarters

ALABAMA

On December 14, 1819, Alabama became the twenty-second state to join the Union. Alabama was named after an Indian tribe found in central Alabama when explorers first arrived. The name "Alabama" is found in the chronicles of the explorer de Soto from his 1540 expedition. During the Civil War, Alabama seceded from the Union in 1861. The capital of Alabama, Montgomery, served as the first capital of the Confederacy.

Industries in Alabama include iron, steel, lumber products, and chemicals. Agricultural products include cotton, soybeans, and peanuts. Alabama is home to the largest space museum in the world, the Alabama Space and Rocket Center located near Huntsville. Huntsville is known as the "rocket capital of the world," and the rockets made to put Americans on the moon were made in this state. With its beaches along the Gulf of Mexico, Alabama is a favorite vacation spot.

MAINE

Maine became the twenty-third state to join the Union on March 15, 1820. Maine was part of the territory explored by Samuel de Champlain in 1604. The first English colonists settled in Maine in 1607. Maine was part of Massachusetts until it was admitted as a free state under the Missouri Compromise. Maine is the most eastern state, and Eastport, Maine, is the most eastern city in the United States. The top of Maine's Mt. Katahdin is the first place in the U.S. that the morning sun's rays hit.

Maine is approximately ninety percent forested and has thousands of lakes and rivers, creating a paradise for hunting, fishing, and tourism. Maine is also known for its lobsters, wood products, potatoes, and shoes. Maine produces ninety percent of our nation's supply of toothpicks.

MISSOURI

NICKNAME: **SHOW-ME-STATE** • STATE FLOWER:
HAWTHORN • STATE BIRD: **BLUEBIRD**

Jefferson City

Missouri became the twenty-fourth state to join the Union on August 10, 1821. It was admitted as part of the Missouri Compromise of 1820. Missouri was named after an Indian tribe who lived along the Missouri River. Missouri means "people who have canoes." Missouri is often called the "Gateway to the West" because it was located on the edge of the frontier. The Sante Fe Trail, Oregon Trail, and the Pony Express all began in St. Joseph, Missouri.

In 1820, there were twenty-two states in the Union—eleven who were for slavery and eleven who were against—giving equal representation on the issue in the Senate. Admitting Missouri, however, would mean that the balance of power would be shifted to the slave states. Then Maine requested admission as a free state, allowing the Senate to admit both and maintaining the balance of power. This agreement is known as the Missouri Compromise.

The Gateway Arch, which is the tallest man-made monument in the country, is located in St. Louis. Important Missouri industries include beer, tobacco, and horses. Famous people born in Missouri include Harry S. Truman, Walter Cronkite, and Mark Twain.

ARKANSAS

NICKNAME: **THE NATURAL STATE** • STATE FLOWER: **APPLE BLOSSOM** • STATE BIRD: **MOCKINGBIRD**

Arkansas, the twenty-fifth state, joined the Union on June 15, 1836. Arkansas was first settled by the Caddo, Osage, and Quapaw Indians. In 1541, Spanish explorer Hernando de Soto explored the area. In 1682, French explorer Robert La Salle claimed the area for France. The region went back to Spain in 1763, and then back to France in 1800. Arkansas came to the U.S. as part of the Louisiana Purchase of 1815.

Arkansas has the only active diamond mine in the United States, and the diamond is the state's official gemstone. Arkansas draws millions of people each year to its parks, hot springs, and historic sites. Hot Springs, Arkansas, is home to many of this state's famous thermal springs and has long been a favorite destination for celebrities who want to relax or experience their health benefits.

MICHIGAN

NICKNAME: **WOLVERINE STATE** • STATE FLOWER: **APPLE BLOSSOM** • STATE BIRD: **ROBIN**

Michigan became the twenty-sixth state to join the Union on January 26, 1837. The first permanent settlement in this area was Sault Sainte Marie, established by Father Marquette, a Catholic missionary. Michigan is surrounded by four of the Great Lakes and is the only state divided into two separate land areas, the Lower and Upper Peninsula. The name Michigan comes from the Chippewa word "micigami" which means "clearing."

Battle Creek, Michigan, is known as the "Cereal Bowl of America" because it produces more breakfast cereal there than any other city in the world. Detroit, Michigan, is the center of the auto industry in the United States. Other industries important to Michigan include airplane parts and machine tools. Agricultural products include navy beans, cherries, and Christmas trees. Although Michigan is nicknamed the Wolverine State, there are no longer any wolverines in this state. They were hunted extensively for their fur.

FLORIDA

NICKNAME: **SUNSHINE STATE** • STATE FLOWER: **ORANGE BLOSSOM** • STATE BIRD: **MOCKINGBIRD**

In 1513, Spanish explorer Juan Ponce de León, who was searching for the legendary fountain of youth, discovered this area and claimed it for Spain. He named the new land "La Florida" for the day on which it was discovered, Easter Sunday. "La Florida" comes from the Spanish "Feast of the Flowers" held at Eastertime. Florida was later taken by England, and then recaptured by Spain. The land was turned over to the United States as part of the Adams-Onis Treaty in 1819.

The city of St. Augustine was founded in 1565 and is the oldest permanent city in the United States. With its warm climate and beautiful beaches, tourism is one of the most important industries in the state. Cape Canaveral space center and Disney World are both in Florida, and each draws millions of visitors every year. The Everglades is one of the largest swamps in the world. Florida became the twenty-seventh state to join the Union, on March 3, 1845.

TEXAS

Texas became the twenty-eigth state to join the Union, on December 29, 1845. Texas won independence from Mexico after General Sam Houston defeated General Antonio Lopez de Santa Anna at the battle of San Jacinto. The battle of the Alamo was another famous battle in the War for Texas Independence. From 1836 to 1845, Texas existed as a country called the Lone Star Republic, with Sam Houston as its first president. Texas means "hello friend" in the language of the Caddo.

Texas is the second largest state and has the third largest population. It is the only state to have been ruled by six different nations. These "Six Flags Over Texas" were Spain, France, Mexico, The Republic of Texas, the Confederate States, and the United States. Industries include oil, cotton, cattle, and mineral products. One famous Texas ranch, the King Ranch, is even bigger than the state of Rhode Island!

IOWA

The name Iowa comes from an Indian word meaning "the beautiful land." Iowa's motto is "Our Liberties We Prize, and Our Rights We Will Maintain." The first Iowan settlement was in Dobugie in 1783. This state's name is the only one that begins with two vowels.

Agriculture is important in Iowa; it produces one-tenth of the country's food supply including more corn than any other state. Major industries include livestock, mining, and manufacturing. Iowa's Madison County is famous for its many covered bridges. It was the subject of a bestselling book and hit movie. Iowa became the twenty-ninth state to join the Union, on December 28, 1846.

WISCONSIN

NICKNAME: **THE BADGER STATE** • STATE FLOWER: **WOOD VIOLET** • STATE BIRD: **ROBIN**

Wisconsin became the thirtieth state to join the Union, on May 29, 1848. Wisconsin was discovered by the French explorer Jean Nicolet in 1634 while he was attempting to find a water route from Quebec to China. Wisconsin has 7,446 rivers and streams that end to end would stretch 26,467 miles, or all the way around the earth at the equater! Wisconsin also has over eight thousand lakes and many recreational areas.

Wisconsin is our nation's leading dairy state and is world famous for its cheese. In fact, Wisconsin sports fans are sometimes referred to as "cheese heads" and wear hats in the shape of this food. Industries important to Wisconsin include machinery, paper, furniture, and processed food. The ice-cream sundae was invented in Two Rivers, Wisconsin.

CALIFORNIA

NICKNAME: **THE GOLDEN STATE** • STATE FLOWER: **GOLDEN POPPY** • STATE BIRD: **CALIFORNIA VALLEY QUAIL**

California became the thirty-first state to join the Union, on September 9, 1850. Spanish explorer Juan Cabrillo first explored the area in 1542. In 1769, Franciscan friar Junipero Serra established the first mission at San Diego. The twenty-one missions of the "California mission chain" later became the area's centers for farming and ranching. In 1822, California became a province of Mexico. Around 1841, the first group of United States settlers arrived in wagon trains from Missouri. In 1846, after these and other settlers led the Black Flag Revolt, California was ceded to the United

States. After the discovery of gold in 1848 at John Sutter's sawmill in Coloma, thousands of people moved to the state, and the Gold Rush of the "forty-niners" was on.

National parks in California include Sequoia, home to some of the largest trees in the world, Yosemite, Death Valley, which is 282 feet below sea level, and Mount Whitney, the highest point in the United States. The San Andreas fault, which runs along most of the California coast, causes major earthquakes when there is a movement in the fault. One of these earthquakes destroyed much of San Francisco in 1906. Leading industries in California include electronics, aerospace, tourism, and agriculture.

MINNESOTA

NICKNAME: **LAND OF 10,000 LAKES** • STATE FLOWER: **LADY SLIPPER** • STATE BIRD: **COMMON LOON**

Minnesota became the thirty-second state to join the Union, on May 11, 1858. Minnesota received its name from the Minnesota River, which the Dakota Indians called "mnishota," meaning "cloudy or milky water." After the French and Indian War in 1763, the British claimed most of the land in Minnesota. The land was given to the United States after the Revolutionary War.

Although Minnesota is called the "Land of 10,000 Lakes," it actually has more than ten thousand. Minnesota is the leading producer of iron ore in the country, and its agricultural products include grain, rice, cheese, butter, and sugar beets. This state's Mall of America is the world's largest indoor shopping mall. Minnesota has also given Americans some great breakfast inventions, including Wheaties, Cream of Wheat, and Bisquick. Yum!

OREGON

NICKNAME: **BEAVER STATE** • STATE FLOWER: **OREGON GRAPE** • STATE BIRD: **WESTERN MEADOWLARK**

Oregon was the thirty-third state to join the Union, on February 14, 1859. It was originally part of the Oregon Territory.

The Oregon Territory was made up of land north of California and west of the Rocky Mountains. During the early nineteenth century, this area was occupied by both the United States and Britain. American claims for the area were based on the discoveries of Captain Robert Gray, the explorations by Lewis and Clark, and the establishment of Astoria by John Jacob Astor. British claims were based on the discoveries of Sir Francis Drake, Captain James Cook, and Captain George Vancouver. In 1846, the United States and Great Britain signed a treaty dividing the territory and making the forty-ninth parallel the boundary between the United States and Canada.

Oregon has many famous tourist attractions, including Crater Lake, the deepest lake in the United States, Bonneville Dam, and the Columbia Gorge. Oregon's state flag has the crest of the state on the front and a picture of a beaver on the back. It is the only state flag to have two different images on the front and back.

KANSAS

NICKNAME: **JAYHAWK STATE** • STATE FLOWER: **SUNFLOWER** • STATE BIRD: **MEADOWLARK**

Kansas, the thirty-fourth state, joined the Union on January 29, 1861. The name Kansas comes from the Dakota Sioux Indian word "Kanze" which meant "people of the south wind." Between 1854 and 1861, Kansas was divided over the issue of slavery. In 1854, the Kansas-Nebraska bill created the Kansas and Nebraska Territories, allowing settlers from each territory to decide if the state would be free or slave. Settlers who believed in both sides of the issue poured in to settle the state and cast their votes for freedom or slavery. These settlers fought about the issue until slavery was ended by the Civil War.

Kansas is the nation's leading producer of wheat and is one of the country's leading manufacturers of nonmilitary aircraft.

WEST VIRGINIA

NICKNAME: **THE MOUNTAIN STATE** • STATE FLOWER:
RHODODENDRON • STATE BIRD: **CARDINAL**

West Virginia became the thirty-fifth state to join the Union, on June 20, 1863. West Virginia was originally part of Virginia. During the Civil War, the western part broke away to remain with the Union, while the rest of Virginia joined the Confederacy. West Virginia is the only state to have been directly given its independence through a declaration by our nation's president. It is considered both as the northernmost southern state and the southernmost northern state.

West Virginia is covered with scenic mountains and hills attracting many tourists each year. Industries include coal mining, tobacco, lumber, chemicals, glass, and steel. West Virginia was the first state to declare Mother's Day. It first celebrated the holiday in 1908.

NEVADA

NICKNAME: **SILVER STATE** • STATE FLOWER: **SAGEBRUSH**
• STATE BIRD: **MOUNTAIN BLUEBIRD**

In 1848, the Mexican government gave Nevada to the United States. In 1859, thousands of people moved to Nevada in search of gold and silver after the discovery of the Comstock Lode. The name Nevada comes from Spanish sailors who saw the mountain ranges from out at sea and named them Sierra Nevada, or "snowy range." Nevada became the thirty-sixth state to join the Union, on October 31, 1864.

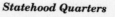

Las Vegas is called the entertainment and gambling capital of the world. Forty-five percent of Nevada's revenue comes from gambling taxes, and in 1999, there was one slot machine for every ten residents of this state. Nevada's Hoover Dam was the world's highest concrete dam for many years. Construction lasted between 1930 and 1935 on this huge dam, which provides hydroelectric power for much of the region.

NEBRASKA

NICKNAME: **CORNHUSKER STATE** • STATE FLOWER: **GOLDENROD** • STATE BIRD: **WESTERN MEADOWLARK**

Nebraska became the thirty-seventh state to join the Union, on March 1, 1867. Nebraska became a territory in 1854. In 1842, French explorer Fremont used the word Nebraska in reference to the Platte River, which means "broad river" in French. Nebraska became a state as part of the Kansas-Nebraska Act.

Nebraska has more miles of rivers than any other state. It is a leading farming state with rye, corn, and wheat as its main products. In 1927, Kool-Aid was invented by Nebraskan Edwin Perkins. Spam is also made in this state.

COLORADO

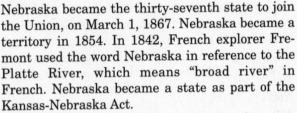

NICKNAME: **THE CENTENNIAL STATE** • STATE FLOWER: **ROCKY MOUNTAIN COLUMBINE** • STATE BIRD: **LARK BUNTING**

The name of our thirty-eigth state means red in Spanish, referring to the color of the Colorado River. Early Native American tribes gave the river this name because of its color, which comes from the area's red clay soil. Colorado was part of the Louisiana Purchase. This state's nickname is "The Centennial State" because it joined the Union on August 1, 1876, a hundred years after the signing of the Declaration of Independence.

Colorado has many natural attractions, including the Rocky Mountains, Pike's Peak, and Mesa Verde and Dinosaur national parks. If you ever go to Colorado, make sure to visit Sand Dunes National Park, which is home to the highest sand dunes in the world. From several miles away, they look small, but it's amazing how enormous they are when you are close and how much fun they are to climb.

Tourism is an important industry in Colorado, especially in snow-skiing season. Other industries include mining, manufacturing, cattle, and sheep herding. The American Numismatic Association, in Colorado Springs, has a great museum to visit where you can learn all about coin collecting and the history of coins.

NORTH DAKOTA

NICKNAME: **FLICKERTAIL STATE** • STATE FLOWER: **WILD PRAIRIE ROSE** • STATE BIRD: **WESTERN MEADOWLARK**

North Dakota became the thirty-ninth state to join the Union, on November 2, 1889. North Dakota's motto is "Liberty and Union Now and Forever, One and Inseparable." North Dakota was part of the territory explored by Lewis and Clark during their expedition. In 1861, North Dakota became a territory, and the land was opened to settlers, pushing Native Americans off their land. This led to fighting between the natives and settlers, but with the surrender of the famous Chief Sitting Bull in 1881, peace was achieved. Sitting Bull Burial State Historic Site, near Fort Yates, is a monument to the life and death of the great Native American leader.

The name "Dakota" comes from a Sioux word meaning "friend" or "ally;" the Sioux nation was made up of the Dakota, Lakota, and Nakota tribes. North Dakota consists of ninety percent farmland. Agriculture and mining are the major industries.

SOUTH DAKOTA

NICKNAME: **MOUNT RUSHMORE STATE** • STATE FLOWER: **AMERICAN PASQUE FLOWER** • STATE BIRD: **RING-NECKED PHEASANT**

South Dakota became the fortieth state when it joined the Union on November 2, 1889 at the same time as North Dakota. Both Dakotas were originally part of one territory called the Dakota Territory. Gold was discovered in South Dakota's Black Hills in 1874, bringing many people to the state.

Mount Rushmore is this state's most famous attraction. Huge sculptures of the heads of four Presidents are carved into this granite mountainside. The four images are of George Washington, Thomas Jefferson, Theodore Roosevelt, and Abraham Lincoln. Each image is sixty feet tall, the largest in the world. Work started on Mount Rushmore in 1927 and was finished in 1941. Other famous South Dakota attractions are the carving of Chief Crazy Horse near Custer and Dinosaur Park. Custer State Park is also the home of one of our nation's largest herds of free-roaming bison. Bison were of great importance to the tribes of the Sioux Nation.

MONTANA

NICKNAME: **TREASURE STATE** • STATE FLOWER: **BITTERROOT** • STATE BIRD: **WESTERN MEADOWLARK**

Montana became the forty-first state to join the Union, on November 8, 1889. In 1876, the battle of the Little Big Horn, also known as "Custer's Last Stand," took place in Montana. Chief Joseph surrendered to the U.S. Cavalry in 1877 at Bear Paw, Montana, ending the resistance of the Plains Indians to the U.S. expansion. The name Montana comes from the Latin word "montaanus," which means mountainous. The Montana Territory was created in 1864 from the Idaho Territory.

Montana is home of many birds and wildlife, including more species of mammals than any other state. Products produced in Montana include gold, silver, copper, lead, wheat, sheep, and cattle. Tourists also love to visit this state's old gold camps, dude ranches, and parks such as Glacier National Park. But be careful in the Montana wilderness—this state has more grizzly bears than any of the other lower forty-eight states, though they rarely bother humans.

WASHINGTON

NICKNAME: **EVERGREEN STATE** • STATE FLOWER: **COASTAL RHODODENDRON** • STATE BIRD: **WILLOW GOLDFINCH**

Washington, the forty-second state, joined the Union on November 11, 1889. Before this state was admitted, the territory was named Columbia. Its name was changed when it became a state so that it would not be confused with the District of Columbia and our nation's capital. It is the only state named for a United States President. Washington State consists of many forests on the west and dry land on the east, separated by the Cascade Mountains.

The 1962 World's Fair was held in Seattle, Washington. The first monorail service in the United States was used there. Also featured was the Space Needle, a 605-foot observation tower and revolving restaurant at the top. Tourism is an important industry, especially with hunting and fishing. The state's main products include apples, lumber, pears, wheat, aluminum, fish, and flower bulbs. Soft-serve ice cream was first invented at a Dairy Queen store in Olympia, Washington.

IDAHO

NICKNAME: **GEM STATE** • STATE FLOWER: **SYRINGA** • STATE BIRD: **MOUNTAIN BLUEBIRD**

Idaho became the forty-third state to join the Union, on July 3, 1890. Congress designated this region as the Idaho Territory in 1863. Congress believed that Idaho meant "gem of the mountains." Located in the Rocky Mountains, Idaho is covered with beautiful mountains and forests. One of the Native American tribes that lived in this region, the Nez Perce of Idaho's Kamiah Valley, bred the first Appaloosa horses for use as war ponies.

Idaho potatoes are a famous and important crop for this state. Tourism also brings many people to the state for fishing, skiing, and other sports. The U.S.'s deepest canyon is Idaho's Hell's Canyon, which divides Idaho and Oregon along the Snake River.

WYOMING

NICKNAME: **EQUALITY STATE** • STATE FLOWER: **INDIAN PAINTBRUSH** • STATE BIRD: **MEADOWLARK**

Cheyenne

Wyoming became the forty-fourth state to join the Union, on July 10, 1890. Wyoming was the first state to give women the right to vote. In 1872, Congress created Yellowstone National Park. It was the first national park in the country. Other popular parks in this state include Grand Teton National Park and Jackson Hole National Monument.

Sometimes known as "The Cowboy State," Wyoming's license plate shows a picture of a man riding a bucking bronco. The horse's name is "Old Steamboat." Cheyenne's annual Frontier Days Rodeo is the world's largest outdoor rodeo. Industries in Wyoming include wool, sheep, cattle, oil, uranium, and natural gas. The idea of having tourists visit a "dude ranch" originated in Wyoming. The first dude ranch was the Eaton Ranch, near Wolf, Wyoming.

UTAH

NICKNAME: **BEEHIVE STATE** • STATE FLOWER: **SEGO LILY**
• STATE BIRD: **CALIFORNIA GULL**

Utah became the forty-fifth state to join the
Union, on January 4, 1896. In 1847, Brigham
Young started a settlement in Utah by leading the
Mormons to an area near the Great Salt Lake. A
year after swarms of crickets started to eat all of
the crops, seagulls from the lake came and ate the
crickets, saving the settlement. Because of this,
the seagull became the state bird.

In 1869, the Transcontinental Railroad met at
Utah's Promontory Point, connecting the East
and West Coasts by rail. The spot is now marked
by the Golden Spike National Historic Site.

Important industries for this state are manufacturing, tourism, and mining. Utah's Rainbow
Bridge, the world's largest natural-rock bridge, is
a span of solid sandstone 278 feet wide and 309
feet high. Utah is known as the "Beehive State"
because its people are hard working, just like bees
in a hive.

OKLAHOMA

NICKNAME: **SOONER STATE** • STATE FLOWER: **MISTLETOE**
• STATE BIRD: **SCISSOR-TAILED FLYCATCHER**

The forty-sixth state is Oklahoma, which joined
the Union on November 16, 1897. The name Oklahoma comes from the Choctaw word meaning
"red people." Between 1830 and 1842, this territory was the final destination of the Trail of Tears,
when the U.S. government forced Native Americans out of the southeastern United States. In
1889, what was this new Indian territory was
opened to settlers. Thousands of people lined up
along the border to claim land. Some "sooners"
moved in on the land before the official date to
begin settlement. These people gave the state its
nickname.

Important Oklahoman products are natural

gas and petroleum. There are many interesting sites of Native American culture to visit in this state, including the Cherokee Cultural Center in Tahlequah. The Cherokee Nation of Native Americans was moved from Georgia to Oklahoma on the Trail of Tears.

NEW MEXICO

NICKNAME: **LAND OF ENCHANTMENT** • STATE FLOWER: **YUCCA** • STATE BIRD: **ROADRUNNER**

•Santa Fe

New Mexico became the forty-seventh state to join the Union, on January 12, 1912. Pueblo Indians originally lived in the area. They lived in cliff dwellings, some of which are still used. In 1881, with the completion of the southern railroad, the territory became linked to the rest of the country. The first atomic bomb was made and tested at Los Alamos, which is still a center of some of our nation's most advanced nuclear research.

The New Mexico Palace of Governors is the oldest public building in the United States. Tourism is very important to this state, and many people come for fishing, hunting, skiing, and sightseeing. Many tourists also come to see Albuquerque's annual Hot Air Balloon Fiesta, the largest hot air balloon festival in the world. New Mexico's famous White Sands National Monument also has an interesting secret—the white sand isn't sand at all, but tiny, tiny crystals of a mineral called gypsum!

ARIZONA

NICKNAME: **THE GRAND CANYON STATE** • STATE FLOWER: **FLOWER OF THE SAGUARO CACTUS** • STATE BIRD: **CACTUS WREN**

•
Phoenix

Arizona became the forty-eighth state to join the Union, on February 14, 1912. The Spanish ruled this region from the 1530s to the early 1800s, when it became part of Mexico. As a result of the Mexican War between 1846 and 1848, the United States claimed the territory of Arizona. During the Civil War, Arizona was occupied by northern troops.

Arizona became a territory in 1863 and was a scene of many conflicts between natives and settlers. The development of irrigation systems helped the soil become rich, and many people moved into the area. The name Arizona comes from two words in the Pima language of the Papago Indians, "Aleh-zon," which means "little spring." This term was first used by the Spaniards around 1736. Arizona's Native American population is the highest of any state.

Arizona's most famous and visited tourist attraction is the Grand Canyon, which is visited by five million people each year. The Grand Canyon covers 1,904 square miles and is eighteen miles across from rim to rim. Some of the rocks at the bottom of the canyon may be as much as two billion years old.

ALASKA

NICKNAME: **THE LAST FRONTIER** • STATE FLOWER: **FORGET-ME-NOT** • STATE BIRD: **WILLOW PTARMIGAN**

Alaska became the forty-ninth state to join the Union, on January 3, 1959. The name Alaska is taken from the Aleut "alaxsxaq," meaning "the object toward which the action of the sea is directed." Alaska was owned by Russia until it was purchased by America for $7.2 million—or two cents an acre!—in 1867. Many Americans thought the land was a silly thing for America to spend its money on and called the purchase "Seward's Folly." The wealth of oil and natural gas since discovered has proved those people wrong.

Juneau

In 1896, the discovery of gold in the Klondike region of the Yukon created a gold rush to the state. Its most important industries are gas, oil, fishing, and lumbering.

HAWAII

NICKNAME: **ALOHA STATE** • STATE FLOWER: **YELLOW HIBISCUS** • STATE BIRD: **NENE**

Hawaii became the fiftieth state to join the Union, on August 21, 1959. It is the only state that is outside North America and is made up of over one hundred volcanic and coral islands. Polynesians first inhabited the islands about two thousand years ago. In 1778, Captain James Cook of England discovered the islands and named them the Sandwich Islands in honor of England's Earl of Sandwich. In 1819, the Kingdom of Hawaii was formed under King Kamehameha. But in 1893, Queen Liliuokalani was deposed in a revolution led by Americans. Hawaii then became a republic with American millionaire Sanford Dole as its president. In 1898, the United States claimed Hawaii as a territory.

In the early 1800s, whalers and traders arrived, bringing more Americans to the islands, but missionaries dominated the area for much of the nineteenth century. In 1942, the Japanese attacked the U.S. naval base at Pearl Harbor, drawing the United States into World War II. Important industries include tourism and sugarcane and pineapple growing.

Fun Current Coins to Collect

Sacagawea Dollar

In 1997, Congress passed the United States Dollar Coin Act, which allowed the making of a coin that was gold in color, the same size as the Susan B. Anthony dollar, and having an edge that could be distinguished from other coins. The Secretary of the Treasury's requirements for the new dollar were that the obverse contained the image of one or more women, that the image not be of a living person, and that the reverse must show an eagle.

The new Sacagawea dollar coin will be the first new coin of the millennium in the United States. Although the coin is being called the gold dollar, there is no gold in this coin. The coin is made of mostly copper and zinc and contains some nickel and manganese. By adding enough zinc to the copper, the coin appears golden in color. This gold color makes the coin easy to tell apart from the quarter, which is a similar size.

The obverse, or "heads," design was created by Glenna Goodacre. Mrs. Goodacre used a real person as a model for Sacagawea, Randy'L He-dow Teton. In 1998, the Mint requested Goodacre to submit a design for the new dollar coin. At the Institute of American Indian Arts Museum in Santa Fe, New Mexico, Mrs. Goodacre asked if there were any young Shoshone women in the area. One of the employees was Miss Teton's mother, who showed Mrs. Goodacre pictures of her three daughters. Mrs. Goodacre contacted Miss Teton, who was twenty-two at the time, and did a sculpture of her image.

The reverse design was created by Thomas D. Rogers, Sr. It

shows a soaring American bald eagle, the symbol of our nation. It is surrounded by seventeen stars, which stand for the seventeen states belonging to our Union in 1804, during the time of the Lewis and Clark expedition.

Sacagawea was a Shoshone Indian girl who was a guide for the Lewis and Clark expedition in 1805. Lewis and Clark were famous Americans who explored land west of the Mississippi for the young United States. These explorers opened the doors for the expansion of the United States to the Oregon Territory. But without the help of Sacagawea, this expedition would likely have been doomed.

Sacagawea is truly an American hero. Born into a Shoshone tribe, she was captured at age eleven by a Hidatsa raiding party. She was later sold into slavery to the Mandan Sioux, who were living in Fort Mandan, North Dakota. She was then gambled away to a French-Canadian fur trader named Toussaint Charbonneau, who made her his wife.

At age fifteen, Sacagawea spoke several Indian languages. At age sixteen, Sacagawea gave birth to a son, Jean Baptiste—nicknamed Pomp—in February of 1805, and in April of that year, she joined the expedition. Being a Native American, she was helpful in obtaining horses, which were very important to the mission. Sacagawea knew about the land the expedition was traveling, parts of which were some of the most rugged of North America. She also taught the explorers how to find edible plants and roots to eat. Later, when the expedition's boat overturned in the Missouri river, Sacagawea, with her son strapped to her back, saved Captain Clark's journals of the first year of the expedition, saving also a part of history.

Sacagawea helped Lewis and Clark's expedition by serving as a translator, diplomat, and symbol of peace to the Native Americans they met. Her presence as a young mother helped the expedition avoid battle with the tribes whose land they passed through, and not a single member of the expedition was lost to a hostile action.

Modern Series of United States Coins

This section describes coins that are still being made at the United States Mint. These are the most commonly collected United States coins. The series are in order from cents through dollars.

You can collect any of these series from pocket change or with help from your family or friends, so have fun and happy hunting!

For each series, the following information is given:

Photographs: Photographs showing the obverse and reverse of the coin.
Designer: Person who designed the obverse and reverse of the coin.
Years Struck: The years in which the coins were struck.
Mints: The Mints where the coins were struck.
History: History of the creation, design chosen, and other facts regarding the coin. Any changes in the design, metal used, or other changes.
Interesting Facts: Facts about the coin or the person shown on the coin.

LINCOLN CENTS

Wheat back reverse   *Memorial reverse*

Designer: Obverse and wheat back reverse: Victor D. Brenner
Memorial reverse: Frank Gasparo
Years Struck: 1909 to present
Mints: Philadelphia, Denver, San Francisco
Mintmark Location: 1909 to present—below date

History: The obverse of the coin shows a picture of President Lincoln, our sixteenth President. This coin was created to celebrate the hundredth anniversary of President Lincoln's birth. President Lincoln was born in Kentucky in 1809. The Lincoln cent is the first United States coin made for circulation that had the picture of a President. A reverse containing the wheat stalks on the side was used from 1909 to 1958. The reverse was changed to celebrate the 150th anniversary of this great President in 1959. The newer reverse has a picture of the Lincoln Memorial.

In 1943, the metal of the Lincoln cent was changed to steel with a zinc coat (gray colored). This was done because bronze (brown colored), which was usually used to make the cents, was needed for bullets for World War II. In 1944, the metal was changed back to bronze.

Facts about President Lincoln: Our sixteenth President is considered by many to be one of our greatest Presidents. Lincoln came from a simple beginning; he was born in a log cabin in Kentucky. He had little schooling, but did a lot of reading and learned everything he could.

He worked hard and became a lawyer. Mr. Lincoln was opposed to slavery and he made many speeches, letting his feelings be known. He ran for the presidency of the United States in 1860 and won. Almost immediately, South Carolina and other Southern states that were for slavery began to leave the Union. On April 12, 1861, the Civil War began when soldiers from this new "Confederacy" of Southern states fired on Union soldiers at Fort Sumter in South Carolina. This was a terrible war, but Lincoln knew it must be fought to save the future of the Union and end slavery in the states.

On April 9, 1865, Confederate general Robert E. Lee surrendered to Union general Ulysses S. Grant. Five days after the end of the war, President Lincoln was assassinated by John Wilkes Booth.

JEFFERSON NICKEL

Silver reverse

Designer: Felix Schlag
Years Struck: 1938 to present
Mints Struck: Philadelphia, Denver, San Francisco
Mintmark Location: 1938–1942—right side of Monticello
1942–1945—silver war-time nickel—
above dome
1946–1964—right side of Monticello
1968–present—below date

History: In 1938, the Treasury Department wanted to replace the Buffalo nickel with a new design. A competition was held to pick the design. The obverse design had to be of our second President, Thomas Jefferson, and the reverse of Jefferson's house, Monticello. The prize was $1,000. In World War II, nickel was needed for bullets. In 1942, the metal was changed from nickel to silver. Both types of metal were used for the nickel in 1942. To tell the difference, the mintmark was moved from the right side of Monticello to over the dome. The silver metal was used from 1942 to 1945. All silver nickels have the mintmark above the dome. After World War II, in 1946, the metal was changed back to nickel, and the mintmark was moved back to the right side of Monticello. In 1968, the mintmark was moved to the obverse below the date.

Facts about President Jefferson: Thomas Jefferson was our third President. Jefferson was not a very good public speaker, but he was truly one of the greatest writers of his time. His letters and articles brought him great fame in America. Because of his writing skills, he was appointed to write the Declaration of Independence. President Jefferson also invented the American money system that we still use today.

Jefferson was the founder of the Republican party. (This

party's name later changed to the Democratic party, which is the same Democratic party we have today.) Jefferson believed that the people of the nation should and could govern themselves. He also believed all children should be educated in schools. During his presidency, he purchased the Louisiana territory, which more than doubled the size of the United States.

Jefferson served two terms as President. He might have been elected again but did not want to appear to be a dictator and believed no President should serve more than two terms. He also succeeded in keeping the power of the government in the hands of the people.

After his presidency, he retired to his home in Virginia. This beautiful home was called Monticello and is pictured on the back side of the Jefferson nickel. During Jefferson's later years, he continued to help our nation grow. He died on July 4, 1826, which was the same day our second President, John Adams, died. It was also exactly fifty years to the day after the signing of the Declaration of Independence.

ROOSEVELT DIME

Designer: John Sinnock
Years Struck: 1946 to present
Mints Struck: Philadelphia, Denver, San Francisco, West Point
Mintmark Location: 1946–1964—left of torch
                              1965–1967—no mintmark
                              1968–present—above date

History: With the death of President Roosevelt in 1945, the Treasury Department wanted to put his portrait on a coin. The dime was chosen and the Mint Chief Engraver, John Sinnock, created the obverse and reverse designs. The obverse is of President Roosevelt, and the reverse is of a torch with an olive branch around it symbolizing peace after World War II. Silver was used for the dimes from 1946 through 1964. Because of the high cost of silver in 1964, the alloy was changed in 1965 to a clad or sandwich combination of copper in the middle, and cupro nickel on the outside. From 1946 to 1964, the mintmark is located to the lower left of the torch. From 1965 to 1967, no mintmark was used. In 1968, the mintmark was moved to the front of the coin over the date.

Facts about President Roosevelt: Franklin Roosevelt was our thirty-second President. Born into a famous family and related to many of the earlier Presidents, Roosevelt was involved in politics from the start. During World War I, he was the Assistant Secretary of the Navy. At a young age he became ill with polio and lost the use of his legs, but this did not stop him. He became governor of New York in 1926 and served through the early 1930s. In 1932, he was elected President. The Great Depression was still affecting the country, and Roosevelt took action. He lobbied Congress to pass laws to help the many people who lost their homes and savings during the Depression. Roosevelt also started many social programs during his "New Deal Administration" to help the common man. Many of these programs provided work to people with no jobs. During this time, much of the nation's roads, bridges, clearing away of trees, and building of dams was done.

Roosevelt was President in 1939 when World War II began. Though he tried to stay out of the war, he was given no choice when the Japanese bombed Pearl Harbor on December 7, 1941. Roosevelt and other Allied leaders led the fight against the Axis powers, but before the war was won, he became ill and died. Roosevelt had served four terms as President. The only President to serve more than two terms, Roosevelt believed it was important for him not to quit because the country was dealing with such difficult times.

WASHINGTON QUARTER

Bicentennial obverse   *Bicentennial reverse*

Designer: John Flanagan, Jack L. Ahr
Years Struck: 1932 to 1999
Mints Struck: Philadelphia, Denver, San Francisco
Mintmark Location: 1932–1954—Below wreath on reverse
1968–present—To right of ribbon on obverse

History: The obverse of the coin shows a picture of President George Washington, our first President. This coin was created to celebrate the 200th anniversary of President Washington's birth. In 1931, the Treasury Department had a contest. The winner was Laura Gardin Fraser, a distinguished sculptor, but Secretary of the Treasury Andrew Mellon refused to allow Miss Fraser to design the new quarter because she was a woman. Mr. Mellon, instead, picked the design of John Flanagan to be used for the quarter.

The reverse design is an eagle on a group of arrows above a wreath. Several changes were made over time to strengthen the design and improve the strike. In 1965, with a shortage of silver, the metal was changed from silver to a clad or sandwich combination of copper middle to a copper nickel outside. To celebrate the bicentennial of the United States in 1976, a new reverse design was used for the quarter and was used for all quarters made in 1975 and 1976. This featured a drummer boy next to a torch surrounded by thirteen stars. All quarters made in these two years are dated "1776-1976." The normal reverse was used again in 1977.

Facts about President Washington: A portrait of George Washington is found on the United States quarter. Washington is considered to be the Father of our Country. He was elected to be our first President in 1789 and served two terms. Many people wanted him to continue a third term, but he believed it was important to step down and allow others to lead this great country.

Washington was born a farmer. When he was twenty-one, he began his military life. During his military career, others realized what a great leader he was because of his ability to inspire his troops.

After the colonies won their independence from England in 1776, many of the colonies considered themselves independent states, and there was fear that they might start fighting among themselves. So in 1787, most of the important leaders in America held a meeting called the Constitutional Convention.

Washington was the chairman of the convention. The Constitution of the United States was drawn up at the meeting and is still the same one that governs us today.

These great men also nominated George Washington to be the President, and he received every vote. During his presidency, he tried to be the leader of all the people. He also tried to avoid being a dictator, but knew that the government could not last unless it could enforce its laws on the individuals and the government.

Washington established what the office of the presidency should be, kept our young country together, and provided a plan for it to grow.

KENNEDY HALF DOLLAR

Bicentennial obverse

Bicentennial reverse

Designer: Gilroy Roberts, Frank Gasparro, Seth Huntington
Years Struck: 1964 to present
Mints Struck: Philadelphia, Denver, San Francisco
Mintmark Location: 1964—below right leg of eagle
1968–present—below bust

History: After the assassination of President Kennedy in 1963, the half dollar was changed to contain his portrait on the obverse. The presidential coat of arms was used for the reverse of the coin and was designed by Frank Gasparro. The obverse was designed by Mint Chief Engraver Gilroy Roberts. Mr. Roberts used the design on President Kennedy's inaugural medal to help get the coin done on time. In 1965, because of the rising cost of silver, the half dollar was changed from silver to a silver clad, or sandwich combination of silver and copper. This was used until 1971, when the metal was changed to copper nickel clad. To celebrate the bicentennial of the United States, the reverse design was changed for the quarter, half dollar, and dollar. The bicentennial reverse for the half dollar, which was designed by Seth Huntington, is Independence Hall in Philadelphia. Coins struck in these three series during 1975 and 1976 contained the doubled date "1776–1976." There are no quarters, halves, or dollars dated 1975.

Facts about President Kennedy: Our thirty-fifth President was the youngest person ever to become President. President Kennedy served in the Navy during World War II. After the war, he began his political career. He was first elected to Congress, then to the Senate, and was elected President in 1961. During his presidency, he developed the Peace Corps to help people in poorer countries. Kennedy was also a leader for civil rights in our country. When he was President, there was still segregation in our country. He worked toward ending this separation of citizens. Unfortunately, his term as President ended suddenly when he was assassinated in Dallas, Texas, on November 22, 1963. He was one of our country's most beloved Presidents.

SUSAN B. ANTHONY DOLLAR

Designer: Frank Gasparro
Years Struck: 1979 to 1981, 1999
Mints Struck: Philadelphia, Denver, San Francisco
Mintmark Location: 1979–1981—left of bust

History: The obverse is of Susan B. Anthony, a leader in women's rights. This was the first coin in which an image of a woman was used on a United States coin. The reverse is the same as was used on the reverse of the Eisenhower dollar, which was created to celebrate the first landing on the moon.

One problem was that this coin was very close in size to the Washington quarter and would sometimes be confused with it.

Other Collectible U.S. Series

Besides the United States coin series currently being made, there are many other series that you can collect and enjoy. Some older coins can be difficult or expensive to collect, so be sure to do a little research before you choose one to start on.

This section covers some popular series that are often collected and that are in the price range of a beginning collector. You will not find many of the coins covered in this section in your pocket change, but your parents or grandparents might have some saved from when they were young.

Description of Information Given for Each Series
Photographs: Photographs showing the obverse and reverse of the coin. The photos are the same size as the coin.
Designer: Person who designed the obverse and reverse of the coin
Years Struck: The years in which the coins were struck.
Mints: Mints where coins were struck.
History: History of the creation, design chosen, and other facts regarding the coin. Any changes in the design, metal used, or other changes.
Collecting: Provides different ways to collect a series. Tells what grades are best to search for and what years are more rare and expensive.

INDIAN CENTS

Designer: James B. Longacre
Years Struck: 1859 to 1909
Mints Struck: Philadelphia, San Francisco

History: In 1859, Chief Engraver James Longacre changed the design of the cent. He chose for the new obverse an "Indian Head," but this portrait is actually believed to be the face of Venus Accroupie, a Greek-Roman god with an Indian headdress. The reverse has a laurel wreath. In 1860, the reverse was changed to an oak wreath with a shield on top. In 1864, an 'L,' for Longacre, was added to the ribbon on the obverse. Because of a shortage of nickel in 1864, the metal of the cent was changed to bronze.

Collecting: This coin was made during a period of great change in our country—the West was being expanded, and new inventions were created that changed the way people traveled and did things. You will not find these coins in circulation, but your grandparents might have saved some. There are several ways to collect this series. Start with 1880 to 1909 in grades of EF-40; the average price will be about eight dollars per coin, and the coin will be in a grade in which you can see a lot of detail. Coins before 1880 can be expensive in this grade, so if you want to put a nice mint-state set of these together, start with coins from 1880 to 1909 in grades of MS-63 Red and Brown. These coins have an average price of about twenty-five dollars. Indian Head cents were red when they were created and can change color to brown. Red coins are worth more than brown. Red-brown Indian cents still have the nice red color but have changed slightly to brown. These are much cheaper but just as nice.

FLYING EAGLE CENTS

Designer: James B. Longacre
Years Struck: 1857 to 1858
Mints Struck: Philadelphia

History: In 1856, because of the rising price of copper, the cost of making the Large and Half cents was more than the face value of the coin. Congress decided to make a new cent. The Mint Chief Engraver, James B. Longacre, used an eagle for the obverse and a wreath for the reverse. The wreath design incorporated images of corn, wheat, cotton, and tobacco, the country's main agricultural products at that time. A few hundred 1856 Flying Eagle cents were made for congressmen. These 1856 cents were not made for the general public and are considered very rare today. In 1857, the coins were produced for the public for the first time. People gathered around the block at the Mint and at banks to trade their old Large and Half cents for the new cents. Many of these new cents were saved by people. This started a whole new generation of coin collectors, as is happening today with the new state quarters.

Collecting: Low-grade Flying Eagle cents can be bought cheaply, but nice uncirculated coins can be expensive. Coin folders and albums usually have the Flying Eagle cent and the Indian cent together as part of a set.

BUFFALO NICKEL

1937D
"3-Leg"
Buffalo nickel

Designer: James Earle Fraser
Years Struck: 1913 through 1938
Mints Struck: Philadelphia, Denver, San Francisco

History: In 1911, Treasury Secretary Franklin MacVeagh wanted to change the design for the nickel. James Earle Fraser was asked to create and submit designs. For the obverse of the coins, Fraser chose a portrait that was a composite of three Native American chiefs: Iron Tail (Custer's opponent at the Little Big Horn), Two

Moons, and John Big Tree. On the reverse, Fraser chose an American bison, Black Diamond, who was living at the Central Park Zoo in New York. Two different reverse designs were used in 1913. On the first design used, known as Type I, it was found that FIVE CENTS at the bottom of the coin wore too quickly. The reverse was changed to put FIVE CENTS below the height of the mound; these are known as Type II and were used for the rest of the series.

Unusual coins: In 1937, one of the Denver dies was polished on the reverse, removing the front right leg of the Buffalo. This is known as the 3-legged variety and is very valuable. This coin can still be found at coin shows and stores. The same type of polishing can be found from dies used for 1913-D, 1917-D, 1927-D, and 1936-D. More of the leg is polished away on the 1937-D.

Collecting: This is one of the more popular series to collect. You will not find these coins in circulation, but check with your grandparents. They might have saved some from when they were young. A low-grade complete set is not very hard to assemble. If you are looking for a mint-state set, start with coins from 1930 to 1938. Coins from 1920 through 1929 can be much more difficult to find and can be very expensive in high grade, especially coins from the Denver and San Francisco mints. Many of the coins struck in the 1920s are also weakly struck.

MERCURY DIME

Designer: Adolph A. Weinman
Years Struck: 1916 to 1945

History: In 1916, the Treasury Department had a competition to redesign the dime, quarter, and half dollar. For the obverse of the dime, Adolph Weinman, the winning designer for the dime and half dollar, used a portrait of Elsia Stevens wearing a winged cap. Many people mistakenly thought the head on the Mercury dime was an image of Hermes or Mercury in Greek folklore. This is why this coin is called the Mercury dime. The reverse design is a Roman *fasces,* an axe bound with a group of rods, which was surrounded by greenery. This design was symbolic of the United States' stance on liberty and justice during World War I.

Collecting: Mercury dimes are an undervalued and undercollected series, which is good for the beginning collector. Less demand means cheaper prices and more coins to choose from. The entire series can be put together with the average price per coin of about one dollar. For a higher-grade collection, collect each date and mintmark between 1934 and 1945 at a grade of MS-63. The average price of these coins will be about ten dollars, and you will have nice uncirculated examples. Try to look for spotless coins.

There are two horizontal bands on the center of the Roman fasces on the reverse. These bands are directly opposite the highest point on the obverse and are often weakly struck. When there is complete separation between the lower and upper band, this is known as "Full Bands" or "FB." If only part of the bands is separated, it is called "Split Bands," and if there is no separation, it is called "Flat Bands." Mercury dimes with full bands are worth much more.

Full Bands   *Split Bands*   *Flat Bands*

EISENHOWER DOLLAR

Bicentennial reverse

Designer: Frank Gasparro, Dennis R. Williams
Years Struck: 1971 through 1978
Mints Struck: Philadelphia, Denver, San Francisco

History: The obverse is Dwight D. Eisenhower, our twentieth President from 1952 to 1960 and one of the greatest leaders of the United States in the twentieth century. He was the Supreme Allied Commander in World War II. The reverse represents the landing on the moon, America's greatest technological achievement in the twentieth century. President Eisenhower was also part of this achievement; he signed the bill into law that created NASA. To celebrate the bicentennial in 1976, the reverse of the quarter, half dollar, and dollar were changed and used for one year. For the Eisenhower dollar, the Liberty Bell over the moon was used.

Collecting: This series is very easy to assemble for all dates for all three mints. These coins can be obtained for a small price at coin shows or stores. Because all coins are inexpensive, it is suggested that you collect this series in high grade. With so many coins available to choose from, take your time and choose the best pieces with no marks or toning.

Key Dates: All dates and mintmarks are relatively easy to obtain.

MORGAN DOLLAR

Designer: George T. Morgan
Years Struck: 1878 through 1904 and in 1921
Mints Struck: Philadelphia, San Francisco, Carson City, New Orleans

History: More than 550 million Morgan dollars were struck between 1878 and 1904. About 490 million of these were put into Treasury vaults, and only about 70 million went into circulation and were used. This means that 90 percent of the Morgan dollars struck were never used.

The Morgan dollar series was created mainly because of politics, greed, and American silver mine owners. The silver dollar is a heavy coin that was not used regularly by the public. In 1873, Congress therefore stopped the production of the silver dollar in the United States. During the 1870s, however, Germany put a lot of silver on the market. At this time in the United States, many new silver mines were opening in the West. These two factors meant that the price of silver fell. Silver miners wanted to keep the price of silver high by forcing the Mint to only buy silver here in the United States. In 1878, with the help of Congressman Richard Bland and Senator William Allison, Congress passed a law that forced the Mint to buy $2 million to $4 million a month in silver for a new silver dollar. The silver miners were paid in gold. By 1893, the Treasury department was almost out of gold, and this caused more than four hundred banks to close. In 1904, coinage of the Morgan dollar was stopped. They were struck again for one year in 1921.

Unusual Coins: None known

The Kid's Guide to Collecting Statehood Quarters

Collecting: This is an extremely popular series, mainly because of the design and availability of the coin. Many coins can be found in mint-state condition. This is because most of the coins struck were put into Treasury vaults. In 1964, many of these coins were sold to the public.

Other Cool Coins to Collect

Collecting Die Varieties

To make a coin, we use a tool called a "die." The die has the image of the coin on it. We need two dies to strike a coin: one for the obverse and one for the reverse. The coins are struck in a machine called a *coining press*. The pair of obverse and reverse dies are placed above and below the coin. The coin is struck by the dies with thousands of pounds of pressure.

To make the dies, there are many steps that the Mint has to take. Sometimes during the die-making process, mistakes can be made. These mistakes can make the die look different from other dies. These are known as *die varieties*. There are many collectors who collect these die varieties. Some types of die varieties are very valuable. Some types are very common during certain years. Below are some examples of different types of die varieties.

A *doubled die* is when there are two or more images on a die. There are many different reasons why these doubled dies are created. Below is a picture of a 1955 Lincoln cent with very dramatic doubling seen all around the coin. This is one of the more dramatic doubled dies for the Lincoln cent series. In perfect condition, this coin can be worth around fifteen thousand dollars. Imagine paying five cents for this coin and selling it for a lot of money. There are thousands of the doubled dies on twentieth-century coins. Many are minorly doubled and worth only a little, but imagine finding a monster like this 1955.

Close-up views of a doubled 1955 Lincoln cent

There are other types of doubling that are not valuable. In these cases, doubling happens when the coin is being struck in the coining press or sometimes when the die wears down. It is important if you want to collect doubled dies to be able to tell the difference between a true doubled die and other types of doubling.

A *repunched date* is when the date was punched into the die more than once. We only see repunched dates on coins that were made before 1909. Before 1909, the date was struck into each die by a Mint person who used a hammer and a date punch. Sometimes he wanted to get a deeper impression into the die or thought it was too high or low. Many of these repunched dates only show minor signs of extra digits. Some are very dramatic and are valuable.

Repunched dates. Can you find the remains of the earlier dates on these coins?

A *misplaced date* is the same as a repunched date, but the repunched digits are much farther away. Sometimes by accident, the digits of the date were punched into the *denticles* below the date or the design of the coin above the date. There are many reasons this could happen, but it is mainly thought that the mistakes were caused by inexperienced Mint employees or by misjudgment. Remember, the area in which the date is struck is only one-quarter of an inch wide and one-tenth of an inch high.

 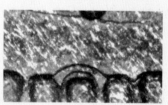

A misplaced date. This coin has part of a 0 peeking out from the denticles.

Overdate coins are very rare. On this coin, a 1917 date has been covered with a 1918.

One of the rarest types of die varieties and sometimes the most valuable is an *overdate*. An overdate is a coin that shows two dates from different years.

A *repunched mintmark* is a coin that shows two or more mintmarks punched into it. Up until around 1990, the mintmark was struck into each die by a Mint employee with a hammer and a punch with the mintmark at the end. If the Mint employee thought the first punch was too soft, too high, or too low, then he might strike the mintmark again into the die. Repunched mintmarks are common for twentieth-century coinage, especially for Lincoln cents. Some of the more dramatic repunched mintmarks can be very valuable.

Can you see the faint D below the D mintmark on this repunched coin?

An *over mintmark* is a coin that shows two or more different lettered mintmarks. Over mintmarks are rare with about fifty known for all series. These are highly collected and sought after.

Look closely and you will see an S mintmark below the D mintmark on this coin.

Collecting Error Coins

Sometimes, when a *planchet,* or blank piece of metal, is fed into a coining press, it is not placed properly between the dies. When this happens, an *error coin* can result.

There are many types of error coins, and there are many books that have been written about them. These are some of the most common errors to look for:

The Kid's Guide to Collecting Statehood Quarters

Off center strikes are one type of error coin.

Double Struck   *Chain Strike*

Capped Die   *Brockage*

Flip Over Double Struck   *Folded Edge Struck*

Collecting Foreign Coins

Collecting foreign coins can also be fun. There are many different ways to collect foreign coins. You can collect one from each country or just collect coins from one country.

Foreign coins are usually readily available and affordable. Even older foreign coins can be much cheaper than United States coins from the same time frame. The most popular and easiest foreign coins to collect are from Mexico, Canada, and England.

Just like in the United States, the images used on foreign coins are famous people, history, places in that country, or perhaps something important. On a coin from the Vatican you could find a picture of Pope Paul II. England uses the images of its kings and queens on many of its coins. Queen Elizabeth II is on many of the British coins used today. The elk is an important animal in Canada and is portrayed on Canada's coinage. A dragon, which is a well-known symbol in China, is used on China's coinage.

You can find foreign coins when you, your family members, or your friends travel to different countries. Coin shows are also usually a good place to find coin dealers who specialize in foreign coins.

Foreign coins often feature people, places, symbols, or animals that are important to that country

Collecting Hobo Nickels

The Buffalo nickel is one of the most loved of all the coins in the United States. Its design is true Americana. The years of its reign, 1913 to 1938, take us through some of the most remarkable periods in the history of the United States, including the first world war, the Roaring Twenties, the Great Depression, Prohibition—times we must not forget.

The Kid's Guide to Collecting Statehood Quarters

Hobo nickels are Buffalo nickels that were modified through carving by the homeless during the early twentieth century. They were traded for meals, a place to sleep, a ride, or other favors. Often the images of loved ones were carved to remember better times. These unique pieces of metal combine the fields of numismatics, art, and history.

Each of the original Hobo nickels is unique and hand-carved, using the design either of the Indian or buffalo as a base and changing it so that it represents another design. The Indian has been changed to show clowns, Amish men, women, other Indians, friends, loved ones, and self-portraits. The Buffalo has been changed to donkeys, men with packs on their backs, and elephants.

If they could talk, Hobo nickels would have stories to tell about the men and women who struggled during that very harsh period in our country. Here are some examples of Hobo nickels.

Hobo nickels, which are Buffalo nickels carved by American hobos in the 1920s and 1930s, show us unique images from America's past.

For more information about Hobo nickels, you can write to The Original Hobo Nickel Society, P.O. Box 38669, Colorado Springs, CO 80937.

Collecting Ancient Coins

Coins have been made for thousands of years. The great thing about ancient coins is that you can see what was important in that country or empire when the coin was made.

A good place to look at ancient coins is in a museum. Coins were an important part of previous civilizations and continue to be just as important today.

The following coins and information are presented with the help of Robert Hoge, the curator at the American Numismatic Association Museum in Colorado Springs, which is a good place to look at ancient coins. The photographs are courtesy of the ANA.

This coin, a silver half "slater," was made around 561–546 B.C. during the time of King Croeus in the Lydian Kingdom, which is part of modern-day Turkey. The Lydian kings were probably the world's first minters of coinage, starting around 650 B.C. Because of the primitive equipment that was used to make these coins, they are not perfectly round.

The coin above was made around 449–413 B.C. in Athens, Greece. It is called a silver *tetradrachm* and was the primary coinage of Athens' Golden Age. This is the most common classical Greek coin and is often called "owls." Athens was the only Greek city with its own silver supply; its coins became widely accepted in trade.

Made around 336–323 B.C. in the Macedonian Kingdom, the front of this coin has a picture of Alexander III, known as Alexander the Great. The coin is a silver tetradrachm struck at the Pella or Thebes mint. Alexander adopted the Athenian coinage system's standard for his own, which was struck in dozens of mints and was used worldwide throughout his empire.

This coin was made around 280–276 B.C. in the Roman Republic. It is part of the *Aes Grave* series of coinage struck at the Rome mint and is called a bronze *quadrans*. The Romans only began to produce coinage some three hundred years after its introduction elsewhere.

This coin was made between 54–68 A.D. It is called a gold *aureus* and was made at the Rome mint. This coin was issued after the great fire and is thought to show Nero's statue of himself. Many millions of coins were minted under the Roman Empire, from a variety of mints scattered through the provinces.

The Second Judean Revolt against Rome took place in what is now modern-day Israel between 132–135 A.D. This coin, minted during that revolt, is called a silver *denarius* or *zuz* and was made at the Jerusalem mint. The Jewish people enjoyed only a brief period of independence, during which they were able to strike their own coins on top of the Roman coins.

The coin shown above was made in China between 618–627 A.D. during the Tang Dynasty, Gao Zu. It is copper "cash," Kai Yuan Tong Bao issue, an important coin that standardized the four-character design of Chinese coins. Square-holed coppers such as this one were cast with few changes other than the words for more than two thousand years.

Terms and Definitions

Business Strike—A coin that is made for general use and circulation.

Circulated—A coin that shows signs of wear from usage.

Cleaning—Removing dirt or something from the coin or altering the coin by cleaning or washing the surface of the coin. This process can damage the coin and decrease its value.

Commemorative Coin—A coin that is not used for business. It is made to celebrate a person or event.

Counterfeit—A fake coin made outside the Mint, or by changing a real coin.

Date—The year the coin was struck, which is required to be on the coin.

Denomination—The numerical name of a series, which is the value of the coin. Example: A two-cent piece has a denomination of two cents.

Denticles—Small raised bumps that are used on the inside of the rim on some earlier series such as the Indian cents.

Design—The main image on the coin. For example, on the Lincoln cent the main image on the obverse would be the image of President Lincoln. On the reverse, it would be the Lincoln Memorial.

Designer's Initials—Initials of the person who created the design for the coin.

Device—Same as the main design on the coin.

Die Crack—If the die cracks when it was being used in the coining press there will be a crack in the die that will show up as a raised crack on the coin. Not seen often on coins today, very common on coins struck in the nineteenth century.

Die Scratch—If the engraver or person taking care of the dies is trying to clean the dies to remove something on the die, he would polish the die with an abrasive. This could cause the die to become scratched.

Die Variety—A working die that is different from other working dies of the same denomination and date because something happened during the creation of the die. This could be as simple as the date position or a die crack, or this could be doubling, repunching, or a number of things that would make it different from other dies.

Doubled Die—A working die in which the design or letters have become doubled during the die creation.

Field—The flat surface of the coin.

Incused—The part of the design on the coin that has been impressed into or below the surface of the coin.

Legend—The words "UNITED STATES OF AMERICA," which is required to be on all U.S. coins.

Mint State—A business strike coin that has never been used in circulation.

Mintage—The number of coins struck in a year for a single denomination.

Mintmark—Tells which mint a coin was struck at. For example: P stands for Philadelphia, D for Denver, and S for San Francisco.

Misplaced Date—Similar to a repunched date, but the digits are punched into the denticles, design, or some place not near where the date should be.

Motto—The words "E PLURIBUS UNUM," which is required to be on all U.S. coins today.

Obverse—Front of the coin.

Over Mintmark—Working die that has the mintmarks of two different mints punched into it.

Overdate—A working die that has two dates of different years punched into it.

Planchet—The blank piece of metal that is struck in the coining press with the design of the coin.

Proof Strike—Specially made coin for collectors. These coins are not made for circulation. They usually have a mirror field, and a strong strike.

Relief—The design on the coin that is raised or above the surface of the coin.

Repunched Date—Working die in which the date was punched into the die more than one time, showing more than one set of digits.

Repunched Mintmark—Working die in which the mintmark has been punched in more than one time.

Reverse—Back of the coin.

Rim—This is the outer raised portion of the coin. It helps protect the design from wear.

Series—All coins from the same denomination and same design. For example: The Lincoln cents is a series.

Uncirculated—A coin which shows no sign of wear.

The Kid's Guide to Collecting Statehood Quarters

Bibliography

American Numismatic Association. *Official A.N.A. Grading Standards for United States Coins.* 1987.

Breen, Walter. *Walter Breen's Complete Encyclopedia of U.S. and Colonial Coins.* New York, New York: Doubleday, 1988.

Bressett, Kenneth. *The Whitman Guide to Coin Collecting, A Beginner's Guide to the World of Coins.* New York, New York: St. Martin's Press, 1999.

Flynn, Kevin. *Getting Your Two Cents Worth.* Kevin Flynn and Robert Paul, 1994.

Flynn, Kevin. *A Collector's Guide to Misplaced Dates.* KCK Press, 1997.

Flynn, Kevin and John Wexler. *The Authoritative Reference on Lincoln Cents.* KCK Press, 1996.

Flynn, Kevin, John Wexler, and Bill Crawford. *The Authoritative Reference on Eisenhower Dollars.* Archive Press, 1998.

Flynn Kevin and Edward Fletcher. *The Authoritative Reference on Eisenhower Dollars.* Archive Press, 1998.

Flynn, Kevin and Edward Fletcher. *The Authoritative Reference on Three Cent Nickels.* Stanton Publishing, 1999.

Flynn, Kevin. *Morgan Dollar Overdates, Over Mintmarks, Misplaced Dates and Clashed E Reverses.* Archive Press, 1998.

Flynn, Kevin, John Wexler, and Ron Pope. *Treasure Hunting Buffalo Nickels.* Stanton Publishing, 1999.

Flynn, Kevin and John Wexler. *Treasure Hunting Mercury Dimes.* Stanton Publishing, 1999.

Flynn, Kevin and Bill VanNote. *Treasure Hunting Liberty Head Nickels.* Stanton Publishing, 1999.

Fivaz, Bill. *Helpful Hints for Enjoying Coin Collecting.* Stanton Publishing, 1999.

Fivaz, Bill and J. T. Stanton. *The Cherrypickers' Guide to Rare Die Varieties.* Third Edition. Wolfeboro, New Hampshire: Bowers & Merena Galleries, Inc., 1994.

Rudy, James. Photograde. Wolfeboro, New Hampshire: Bowers & Merena Galleries, Inc., 1998. Taxy, Don. *The U.S. Mint and Coinage.* ARCO Publishing Company, 1966.

Wexler, John. *The Lincoln Cent Doubled Die.* Newbury Park, California: Devine Printing Co., 1984.

Wexler, John and Tom Miller. *The RPM Book.* Newbury Park, California: Devine Printing Co., 1983.

Wexler, John and Kevin Flynn. *The Best of the Washington Quarter Doubled Die Varieties.* Stanton Publishing, 1999.

Yeoman, R.S. and Kenneth Bressett, ed. *A Guide Book of United States Coins,* 51st Edition. Racine, Wisconsin: Wextren Publishing Company, Inc., 1998.

ANA MEMBERSHIP APPLICATION
818 North Cascade Ave
Colorado Springs, CO 80903-3279

Junior Membership Dues:
(17 years old and younger)—$11.00

Name _____
Date and Year of Birth _____
Address _____
City _____ State ____ Zipcode ____

I agree to abide by the American Numismatic Association bylaws and Code of Ethics which require
the publication of each applicant's name and state.

[ ] Check here if you DO NOT want your name and address forwarded to the ANA Representative in your area.

[ ] Check here if you would like your name provided to companies with offers we feel may interest you.

_____
Signature of Applicant

_____
Signature of Parent or Guardian

Send payment of $11.00 to American Numismatic Association
818 North Cascade Ave., Colorado Springs, CO 80903-3279

The Kid's Guide to Collecting Statehood Quarters